13/18.

They Two Shall Be One

They Two Shall Be One

Monogamy in History and Religion

Susan Dowell

Collins
FLAME

William Collins Sons & Co. Ltd
London . Glasgow . Sydney . Auckland
Toronto . Johannesburg

First published in Great Britain in 1990 by Flame

Flame is an imprint of
Collins Religious Division,
part of the Collins Publishing Group
8 Grafton Street, London W1X 3LA

Copyright © 1990 Susan Dowell

Printed and Bound by Bell and Bain Ltd., Glasgow

Contents

Introduction

"Suddenly one summer monogamy seemed dangerously attractive ... that moment was as frightening as anything I'd ever known. It felt like a leap into faith to dare to be close again to ... the man with whom I'd once been so intimate, who had then become my enemy. Doubts gouged me to the bone. Then a sort of airy optimism took over. Gradually I felt again what it was like to be with this man and with no other, and was reminded that, in orgasm with him, I'd never known fear. That was all I had to trust, all I had to go by."

"... if you've created an oasis for yourselves you stay in it. We just have to waddle around in the Garden of Eden up here. As I speak the sunlight is playing on the lemons in the conservatory, the smell of jasmine drifts in. Why should we want to get out of the house? That is our dilemma. It's all for the better that lack of freedom. What would you do with it when you got it?"

"... it seems to Philip that infidelity is rather more rife in town. He leaves Francine safe at home with a very active two-year-old, her friends and their children, the house, shopping and the ironing. There's bound to be problems ... but nothing to do with having affairs. ..." (*Observer*, 15.4.90)

Suddenly last summer when I was commissioned to produce a finished text from the material I'd amassed on the subject, the prospect of writing a book on monogamy was as frightening as anything *I'd* ever known. The cliché "taking the plunge" has taken on a meaning which eluded me before. For one thing, media punditry on this subject has grown into a veritable deluge since I started work. (The testimonies quoted above are taken from yet another newspaper enquiry as to whether "fidelity is back in fashion".) While it is encouraging to be writing about what is clearly a hotly debated issue, I have kept a wary distance from this kind of speculation. Born in 1942, I have already lived through enough "changes in sexual attitudes" to make me giddy. However, while trends do not interest me individuals do, and those quoted here are raising questions about monogamy that are important to me and so serve as the starting point of this book.

My purpose in writing it is not so much to assess the present debate, which I am not anyway equipped to do, being untrained in the relevant disciplines, as to relativize it, to measure the changes of my own lifetime against the broad sweep of history. My hope is that a picture of the background against which the minds and spirits of past ages have wrestled with questions of sexual 'rules, roles and relations' – to use the sociologist's terms – will be useful to people wrestling with them today.

We always talk of having a sexual "past" in individualistic – usually negative – terms: in no other area of human life, it would seem, are we so cut off from the interaction of social and cultural ideas that shape our private and public lives today.

On some levels this is inevitable. It is only since the nineteenth century that Western society has had access to either the information or the language to describe sexual experience in any empirical way. A striking feature of the "new" monogamy is that it comes from openly, considering, and in some cases living out, alternatives which were also, until recently, unavailable to most people. But however recent our sexual awareness is I have found that each stage of the past opens out on to landscapes which modern understanding can illuminate.

What was needed, it seemed to me, was not another history of marriage – there are plenty of those and many are useful – but something much more basic: a history of monogamy itself. Where does it come from this equation of sexual exclusiveness with virtue and maturity? – an idea honoured, it would seem, as much in the breach as in the observance. Friedrich Engels who first and most influentially located the origin of monogamy in the "Descent of Woman" (as Elaine Morgan titled her (1972) book on evolution) and the rise of private property, nevertheless judged it to be "a great historical advance". There is a paradox here.

Monogamy may have begun in bio/sociological necessity but the dramatic reversals and fluctuations it has undergone are, as Elaine Morgan points out, more typical of cultural patterns than biological ones, which is why I, along with Morgan, prefer the cultural term "monogamy" to the pseudo-biological "pair-bonding". I examine the ideal alongside the literary and social forms which have evolved to contain and express it – of which the institution of marriage is only one, and one that was for many centuries in conflict with the ideal of true, faithful love – as well as challenge it.

I have tried to restrict myself to material that has been particularly influential in – or reflective of – its age. But a chronology which runs from Old Testament times to the present day is bound to be, in the words Jane Austen applied to her own efforts at history, both "partial and prejudiced". I can best explain my sources and interests by saying something about myself.

I am a Christian and a feminist. Two great traditions, both with a good deal to say about sex; in fact it would be hard to write a book without reference to either. This book, though, is an insider's not a reference book. Those of us rooted, in faith, in both traditions have found that each challenges the limits imposed by the other's discourse, and that the engagement is an exciting, hope-filled and creative one. I hope and pray it may be so for the reader.

Biblical/theological speculation on sex is not always welcome. AIDS has revived some of the most unattractive repressive aspects of Christianity. We have even been told, as people were told when syphilis first reached epidemic proportions, that disease shows us "the finger of God" raised in judgement. If this is God's finger, some wag asked, what does the rest of Him look like? – a question demanding a more serious answer than is customarily offered in this context.

The present AIDS crisis, a sense that the "sexual revolution" may have run its course, has produced a more moderate, respectable but equally ill-founded triumphalism among Christians. It is not uncommon to hear that Christianity has – indeed is – "the answer to AIDS". (The liberal Roman Catholic marriage expert Jack Dominian's recent book – *Sexual Integrity*, DLT 1988 – is thus subtitled.) If the Church is to maintain, as it does, that its teachings reflect an accumulation of human wisdom it cannot maintain its present legalistic a-historical approach to this – or any other – question. For example, the claim that the Church has always "upheld" the value and integrity of marriage is clearly untenable in light of the Church's long exaltation of virginity.

It is often said that the Church simply pays too much attention to sex, to the exclusion of other aspects of human behaviour. I would rather say that the Church pays not too much but the wrong *kind* of attention. One legacy of the long preoccupation with virginity was that Christian thought neglected and distorted its own biblical, God-given sexual symbolism. The dangers facing our planet today, loneliness and alienation, political and economic oppression, ecological decay – and AIDS is a visible sign of all of these – can only be fully grasped when they are seen as arising not just from "secular" hedonism and materialism but from a deeper *de*valuing of material, bodily life which has been perpetuated by the Christian Church.

The modern Church in both its liberal and conservative forms continues (possibly from embarrassment at its purient, sex-obsessed past) to neglect its own central sexual symbolism – one of the best ways of teaching people what "the rest of Him looks like" – and the urgent task of reclaiming and transforming these symbols (by, for instance, including Her in Him!) and opts for the distinctly less illuminating idiom of sociology. Unhistorically and dangerously, since it is conservative status quo social theories and institutions that the Church is most often asked to "uphold" today. While fifteen years ago there was much talk about changing patterns and expectations in marriage – which at least acknowledges that change occurs, sometimes for the better, and that the Church serves people better when it listens to them – this debate has been abandoned in favour of a campaign to return to "biblical" standards of family life. Leaving aside the question of whose standards – Abraham's perhaps? – the assumption that there was a biblical pedigree for the modern nuclear family provides a blatant example of the way defective history leads to defective theology.

My contention is that the Church has best maintained its sexual and doctrinal integrity when it resisted being "conformed to the world". Today this means resisting its enclosure, imposed and/or adopted from the eighteenth century onwards, in the domestic sphere from which it is required to guard the nation's private purity, while leaving the nation undisturbed in its "real" business.

The secularization of public life has not, however, proceeded in the manner predicted at the beginning of this century. Susan Sontag notes in *AIDS and its Metaphors* a broad tendency in our culture, an "end of an era feeling", that AIDS is re-inforcing; an exhaustion for many, of purely secular ideas. The Bible has of course retained its powerful hold over our imagination: biblical language and imagery spring naturally to mind. What better image than the "Garden of Eden" for this longing for a lost age of innocence?

Alongside this conservative sentimental tendency another has emerged to challenge it: the Christian faith has become a vehicle of protest, a means whereby people envision possibilities for changing the conditions under which they live their private and public lives. Liberation theology has been born from the struggles of the poor against unjust political and economic structures, of feminists against male dominance and, more recently, the campaigns launched by environmentalists against the violation of the earth itself. This theology is not, as is asserted by its critics, "new" at all, but arises from a radical re-appropriation of biblical tradition. Here Eden has become a place to be reclaimed, rebuilt, for us all, not just for cosy couples to waddle around in. It is this theology that connects my feminist to my Christian hope.

Feminism is no stranger to biblical imagery; or to the biblical teaching of God as the author of monogamy: although few would count themselves on the friendliest of terms with Him. History shows that biblical "tradition" – which enshrined a double-standardized monogamy – combined with the domestic enclosure of women in Western bourgeois society has both denied women's moral agency in society and atrophied their personal development. Philip and Francine have pinpointed the double-standard that pervades (his) sophisticated urban world. While sympathizing with their determination to enshrine truer and more human values in their home, I also see the need for a wider perspective on "the problems" they realistically foresee. The two worlds they inhabit would be unrecognizable to their fore-mothers and -fathers and their contemporaries in poorer parts of the world; even to some of my neighbours here in rural Shropshire. The suburban domestic isolation in which Francine finds herself isn't "normal" or natural, as both Church and Society often assume.

There is, inevitably, a certain tension between monogamous revivalism and our feminist aspirations. This tension is explored in Marsha Rowe's thoughtful contribution to the *Observer* debate (see above). Rowe, a pioneer feminist activist (one of the collective who inaugurated *Spare Rib* magazine), speaks of marriage as a "stepping off point", of her delight in being able to love passionately and committedly without illusions and phoney romance. "We had deconstructed marriage. It was up to us to reconstruct it our way." Despite some hesitation in imposing my biblically-minded perspectives on a sister's experience I have to say that as I see it "deconstructing" marriage was very much part of the new social order as envisioned by our earliest Christian forebears. The peace Rowe seeks in her faithfulness to the "ultimate someone I love", seems akin to the peace St Paul wished for the saints. Rowe's need to feel supported by the institution instead of threatened by it is resonant with echoes from the past. Better marry than burn?

If we see the Christian experiment with freedom as a new one, which when measured against the sweep of history it most certainly is, it becomes easier to see our own sexual dilemmas as part of a universal human drama, whose meaning and message is still unfolding and whose end is not yet clear but in which, if we choose so to believe, God is working God's purpose out. Someone once said – apropos feminism and its ambivalent relationship to sixties' permissiveness – that we had to be able to say "yes" before we could creatively say "no". Can we not view our ascetic past as an attempt, not as it turned out a very happy or successful one either, to establish a way of saying "no", so that "yes" could really mean what God intended?

The best achievements of feminism lie in its insistence that "private" ethical choices are always socially and culturally constructed. Feminist theology, at its best, applied this principle to its own sources. I am arguing here for the re-centring of questions of sexual behaviour away from the (secularized) sphere of "private" morality and social pragmatism back within the forms and context of the biblical world-view, in which foundational sexual/moral/social constructs – like monogamy – originally arose.

By showing us the first stages of patriarchal ascendance in the human world, the Old Testament is a primary text of feminist analysis. But if we look beneath and outside the texts we discern the power of earlier female-dominated symbols and beliefs that were denied and repressed by biblical patriarchy. In other words, the question of the "inevitability of patriarchy" was a live issue in the ancient world not just a preoccupation of late twentieth century feminists. The dramatic shifts in world consciousness were most directly apparent in sexual relationships, and in the language and forms in which the Bible's sexual teaching is handed down to us today.

Liberation theology seeks to liberate the Good News core of biblical revelation from the false modes of interpretation, sexism, classism and imperialistic pretensions in which they have become trapped. This can be applied – and it is the insider's task so to do – as fruitfully to sexual as to political morality. And there *is* good news. Sex, marriage and child-bearing teach us our place in the order of creation: but they also provide a means, though not the only one, whereby we share as co-workers in God's act of creation.

Biblical thought does not separate "private" and public morality along the lines imposed by our own culture, and this itself can be inspiring and instructive. By re-entering – and re-appropriating – the whole tradition, text and context we can participate in its central praxis and process, which is one of penitence and regeneration. Prophets like Hosea – whose writings I focus on in chapter 1 – tell us that the proper response to tragedy is a change of heart not a change of strategy. The Bible stands in judgement on those who would heal our own tragedy of AIDS by promoting condoms and cosy coupleism. (Jack Dominian's book referred to earlier provides a worrying example of Christian pragmatism in response to AIDS. The author argues that by releasing unhappy and sexually deprived people into the pool of potential promiscuity divorce must now be seen as a far more serious moral danger than abortion. It is hard to see how this can be reconciled with Dominian's Roman Catholicism, which unequivocally stresses the pre-eminence and sanctity of life itself.) Seek ye first the Kingdom of God ... and all these things will be added unto you. I believe that our society's political and sexual integrity has been best defended by those who have pushed at the false boundaries between private and public.

I am, it may be gathered, highly suspicious of calls for a return to the "traditional" standard of Christian monogamy as presently expounded in Church or society. But there are many urgent reasons why we should refuse to cede this territory to "the enemy".

I am convinced that it is when we contemplate "eternity" in our sexual unions; that is, when the experience of whole-hearted, passionate love presses us towards affirming the intensity and meaning of the experience by seeking fidelity and permanence, that we are brought up against the spiritual dimensions of our sexuality.

Sexual fidelity was the element which welded sacred and secular ideas of love together in Renaissance times. Today this is happening in the movement for Gay Liberation. Homosexual Christians are asking for more than tolerance and understanding (though both seem in notably short supply at present): they are asking for the Church's formal blessing on their union. The pledge to fidelity and permanence forms the central platform of the case for gay marriage.

While much of what I have to say is highly critical, since I continue to perceive traditional morality to be largely founded upon male perceptions and reflecting male interests, I nevertheless see it as profoundly and particularly important for Christian feminists to bring their own perspectives to bear on the present debate on biblical sexual teaching. Feminism encompasses moral constructs – indeed *is* a moral construct. Feminists' passionate insistence that the "personal is political" ensures that we see human sexuality to be a central means of understanding and integrating the urgent moral concerns which the world must face if it is to survive the next century.

For the feminist who wishes to integrate these insights with the demands of the Gospel, rooted in the thought-forms of Jewish prophecy and scripture, sexuality is far more than a matter of personal morality. It takes us into the political arena: it makes us join forces with peace-builders and environmentalists in refusing to allow ourselves to be side-tracked, marginalized, pigeon-holed. The justice we pursue is found in the wholeness of a personal/political, spiritual/material worldview. Here, as always, eternity is in love with the productions of time.

*

I would like to thank Graham Dowell, Linda Hurcombe, Sara Maitland, Rosemary Ruether, Giles Semper (my editor at Collins), Angela West and Joy Williams, whose wondrous productions of affection, wisdom and encouragement have been invaluable to me in writing this book.

SD
Summer 1990

1

A Jealous God

For this, for this the envious gods deny us immortality. (Helen Waddell, *Peter Abélard*)

The first class antagonism which appears in history coincides with the development of the antagonism between man and woman in monogamous marriage, and the first class oppression with that of the female sex by the male. Monogamy was a great historical advance, but at the same time it inaugurated, along with slavery and private wealth, that epoch, lasting until today, in which every advance is likewise a relative regression, in which the well-being and development of the one group are attained by the misery and repression of the other. It is the cellular form of civilized society, in which we can study the nature of the antagonisms and contradictions which develop fully in the latter. (Friedrich Engels, *The Origin and History of the Family, Private Property and the State*).

Marriage and monogamy begin inauspiciously in our mythic past, in lost innocence and the wrath of the gods.

There are two leading myths of Paradise Lost in Western culture. In the Classical version Zeus, father of the gods, creates the treacherous, beautiful Pandora and gives her as wife to Epimetheus to punish humanity for receiving the stolen goods of fire and thereby attempting to usurp the power of Olympus. Chaos, evil and finitude are loosed upon the world as Pandora's marriage portion.

In the biblical account the domestic burdens of marriage are laid upon the first humans as a consequence of their Fall. Given to each other, in joy, at the Creation they sought forbidden knowledge so that they too could "be as gods". A flaming sword bars their way home to the primal harmony of the Garden and the Tree of Life itself. Eve brings forth her children in sorrow out of her desire for Adam, her husband, and his "rule over her". Here again it is in her appearance as "wife" that woman is first the curser and the accursed of man. His trouble and strife.

In Engels' version of its origins (quoted above) monogamy appears not in the beginning but as a new stage in human evolution marking "the proclamation of a conflict entirely unknown in prehistoric times". The conflict arose not between gods and humankind but within the human community as it emerged from its prehistoric state:

> It was the first form of the family based not on natural but on economic conditions, namely, on the victory of private property over original naturally developed common ownership. The rule of the man in the family, the procreation of children who could only be his, destined to be the heirs of his wealth – these alone were frankly avowed by the Greeks as the exclusive aim of monogamy. For the rest it was a burden, a duty to the gods, to the state and to their ancestors, which just had to be fulfilled.[1]

Till the mid-nineteenth century myth sufficed as an "explanation" of marriage. Darwin's evolutionary theories may have upset Victorian man's idea of his place in the scheme of things but it was pretty well taken for granted that however He evolved, She came along too as his mate. Early evolutionists did not pay much attention to the relationship between them. Marxists did and their findings were put together in Engels' foundational study. But it is only in the late twentieth century that this text has come into its own.

Before we consider why this is so and what we should make

of it there is one important point that must be made. Till recently studies in the origins of human social forms were anyway the province of the "specialist". In my (grammar school) day only "A" stream children studied Classical languages or mythology in any depth. The school history syllabus moved rapidly on from stones, bones and early nomads to the landscape of dates, lineages and important battles, leaving the undergirding framework of sex/class relations largely unquestioned. This gap has been particularly detrimental for women. Sex relationships define and shape their lives to a far greater degree than men's. Love and marriage, "a thing apart" for men, are "women's whole existence". A woman's moral status rests in her (sexual) purity; in chastity before marriage and absolute fidelity within it. Just as she has been actively discouraged from an intellectual grasp of the history and function of marriage she is further discouraged from locating the requirement of sexual fidelity within the whole spectrum of human ethics. Hers not to reason why, hers but to do or, in many cases quite literally, die.

Many women today both in and out of the feminist networks have come to see women's enclosure in monogamy as the primary location of female subordination, and so they have pressed for a more comprehensive understanding of its roots in history and culture. Engels' data have become of interest to a far wider section of society than ever before, even for those who reject its Marxist base and application. Despite the backlash against it feminism is a widespread and popular movement and as such has challenged both the esoteric nature and the rigid separation of those disciplines which yield a knowledge of the ancient world.

1   Anthropological, linguistic and archaelogical studies.
2   Studies in mythology, the dramatic stories by which people have described their experiences.
3   Theology or, more properly, theogony: the evolution of

the God or Gods who give sacred significance to this experience.

"Women's studies", formal and informal, in all these fields have exposed the androcentric bias of previous (largely male) scholarship, which has considerably distorted our understanding of the development of human culture.

My own entry into the field is through the third of these – theology (and for reasons given above and below I make no apology for my lack of formal training therein). I met the challenge of feminism as a believing Christian and found it to be the critical bridge between faith and politics that I had been seeking. The specific and systematic exclusion of women from the processes of theological reflection as well as the elimination of female experience from its sources has been intensively documented in recent years. More importantly the growth of Liberation Theology bears witness to the transforming power of theology and Bible study as an analytical tool in the hands of those previously denied them. This is particularly welcomed by women; even those who have no personal engagement in biblical faith but have come to see the degree to which its stories and symbols have reinforced the misogyny in Western culture. The Genesis version of our origins has embedded itself in our consciousness, shaping our language and imagination, even, as Kate Millett writes, "in a rationalist era which has long ago given up literal belief in it", while maintaining its emotional assent intact.[2]

The impact of this assent reverberates most directly in those areas of our lives where the Bible's authority is strongest, that is, in its sexual ethical teachings, whose foundational precept – monogamy – is precisely that which women have identified as the source of our oppression! This is the area the church is most often required to pronounce upon today. (How often does our government elicit or welcome a Christian response to issues of economic or foreign policies?)

Our assent to this teaching is of course more than just "emotional". Judaeo–Christian tradition and the moral traditions that have arisen from it have promoted monogamous marriage as the base of a civilized society. While few of the world's people have time or energy left over from the struggle for existence to make an abstract moral good of social necessity, monogamy continues to be upheld in the First World as meeting two essential human needs: that of children for nurture and stability, and individuals' primary need for emotional security. The church claims the threefold authority of Scripture, tradition and their combined grace in enriching social good with spiritual meaning. Monogamy, we are taught, represents an accumulation of human wisdom, safeguarded by faith.

But it is not always and everywhere regarded as an emotional necessity. There is a history of human sentiment which is as diverse, dramatic and perplexing as the sweeping changes of history itself though much harder to pin down. We do however know for certain that "Love and marriage" have not and do not always "go together" like the "horse and carriage" I remember from a rather silly song of my childhood. Professor Lawrence Stone (author of a major historical survey on Family Sex and Marriage) has suggested that the premodern couple protected themselves against the harshness and uncertainty of life by investing very little emotion in each other or their children: the feelings of husband and wife for each other are simply irrelevant to the stability and survival of most marriages, past or present.

The social desirability of monogamy is mutable too. As we saw in the (1988) Anglican Lambeth Conference the church accepts the fact that it can be and is made subject to the more pressing exigencies of economics. The conference decided that polygamous men who wished to become full communicant members of the Church would not be required to put away those "spare" wives who would, it is fair to add, probably starve if they did. We might well ask if Lambeth would have been so sensitive to a culture which practised female polygamy, but then of course we would have to enquire whether a world in which this was a dominant practice would have conferences of all male bishops? Or a Church at all? (This is not an entirely frivolous remark but one way of raising the question I want to discuss in this chapter – the relationship between patriarchal religion and monogamy.)

The "discovery" in the mid-nineteenth century that the patriarchal family is not a primary form at all but one which evolved at a particular stage of human consciousness, has been extraordinarily liberating for women. Patriarchy, as many feminists have remarked, had nearly accomplished the extraordinary feat of passing itself off as "nature". Feminists' investigation of monogamy as a construct of patriarchy seems to me to be entirely valid for, as Engels makes clear, patriarchal ascendance, the subjection of one sex to another, has shaped Western culture. But at the same time as feminist enquiry in this field has been vital to my own thinking, I have come to see it as incomplete. I believe there are considerable dangers in collapsing the ethic of monogamy into the monolithic structure of patriarchy. By doing so we are automatically ruling out (as opposed to *questioning* it, which I believe we should) monogamy's potential for fulfilling important human needs – a potential which, if properly realized, may well outlive patriarchy. Furthermore as a theme in the story of human relations it unfolds in some surprising ways which do not match up to feminist, Freudian, episcopal – or any other – theories of human behaviour.

Since theirs is the religious tradition which has survived to permeate Western culture and language – the very word "patriarchy" derives from the name given to the early leaders of the Old Testament community – they and the tradition they founded have inevitably taken much of "the rap" for sexism. So it is important to keep in mind that this community did not invent patriarchy or, as has already been said, monogamy. They just invented the most influential version of them.

The Hebrew God was in fact the first among his Near East contemporaries to impose monogamy on his chosen people and we see the move towards monogamous marriage proceeding in unique and particular ways in biblical culture. These ways are, as we shall see, directly informed by the transcendent monotheism which forms the core of Yahwist faith and which is throughout invoked as the basis of its sexual ethical teaching. The Old Testament moves on from the pessimism of the Fall narrative to a positive teaching of sexual union and fidelity as a sign of God's covenant with humankind. The God who walked with his children in the cool of Eden's evening did not disappear back to heaven with his privilege and power intact but invested his own purposes in the very couple he had banished therefrom. Adam and Eve's marriage is made into a token and sign of their relationship with their self-confessedly Jealous God, and the failure and betrayals of all conjugal life are considered as the failure of the Creator's own handiwork.

Of course as a Christian I have an interest here, but I have no need to protect it. The kind of Bible teaching most lay people receive gives enormous weight to the positive and unique aspects of its sex ethic; but far too little weight to the cultural context in which this teaching evolved.

The religious cultures of the ancient Near East form the melting pot from which Hebrew writings and Hebrew faith were extracted and furnish some of the earliest verifiable texts of human origins. The great mysteries with which humanity has wrestled from its beginnings – Creation and Fall, male and female, mortality and eternal life – were themes of common currency in the ancient world.

Mythic and scriptural scholarship have long been respectably integrated; a fact which comes as a surprise to many lay people. It certainly did to me, brought up as I was to take or leave the Bible as the undiluted word of God. All but the most rigorous fundamentalists acknowledge the biblical adoption of stories and symbols from other earlier religious cultures. The Noah story, for example, is Babylonian in origin and twentieth century archaeology has shown the Flood to have been a real catastrophe of which people told their own different stories. There were, however, other events of even more momentous significance to which traditional scholarship rarely does justice. First a transition from female-dominated to male-dominated symbol systems which took place in the first two millenia BC.

The question of what went before this change remains speculative. Prehistory yields no developed texts to support feminist dreams of a matriarchal Golden Age or Marxist visions of a pre-capitalist paradise, although we can of course imagine what we will. Throughout the world there is positive archaeological evidence of a period when woman was venerated in several aspects; the primal one being maternal. The correlation between motherhood and woman-power is inescapable and, as the poet Adriennne Rich says, it "worked to endow all women with respect, even with awe, and to give women some say in the life of a people or a clan".[3]

Which brings us on to an another major event – men's discovery of paternity – which shifted the balance of spiritual and political power decisively in men's favour. Rich sees the "discovery" of paternity as coincident with men's first visions of immortality, realizing that "the child she carries and gives birth to is *his* child, who can make *him* immortal, both mystically by propitiating the gods with prayers and sacrifices when he is dead and, concretely, by receiving the patrimony from him".[4] Obviously this discovery occurred at different times among the world's peoples. There are isolated "primitive" societies today which have not made the link between sexual intercourse and pregnancy. These are by no means matriarchal paradises but they do have a very different religious and sexual outlook to our own: male jealousy and the sexual double-standard do not operate in the same ways as they do in patriarchal monotheistic societies.

Male jealousy and sexual double-standards are both strikingly present in the Bible narratives. But I wonder if we realize just how shockingly and aggressively *phallic* the bible's language appears to those who come to it cold. I have met foreign students on Bible-as-literature courses – people for whom it is neither a foundational nor even an influential text – and they are quite revolted by its sexual imagery; by the catalogue of "begats" with hardly a "bore", and particularly by the idea of a God who "opens wombs"! "Great inseminator-in-the-sky" was one irreverent but genuinely shocked epithet. For these students the Bible appears to be little more than a male consciousness newly awakened to its indispensable role in human generation – and making rather a field day of it!

However we come to it there is nothing profane or controversial about seeing the Bible as a patriarchal book. The conspicuous lack of women's "say in the life of the clan" is unarguable. Rich argues that women's cultural invisibility under the institution of marriage came into being "at the crossroads of sexual possession, property ownership and the desire to transcend death".[5] I have some disagreement with the third part of Rich's statement, since as a Christian I do not see the conquest of death as a vain wish-fulfilment but as something that has been wrought, through Christ, for all humanity. But Rich's criteria of sexual possession, property and transcendence – foundational to socialist-feminist critique – should be kept in mind as we look at the development of sexual thought in Old Testament religion.

They were certainly major factors in the Hebrew people's early struggles to retain their own tribal religious identity. Powerful female deities still reigned among their conquered and conquering neighbours, the Egyptians, Canaanites and Babylonians, and so the Bible gives us one of the clearest pictures we have of the conflictual nature of the transition from female- to male-dominated symbols.

The Hebrew people did not storm out of Egypt into Canaan fully clothed in the monotheistic certainty and moral rigour we see depicted on C. B. de Mille celluloid. A long and chequered history lay behind and before them: a history of struggling to come to terms with their strange destiny and their stern, jealous God. We can only begin to make sense of this history if we have some idea of how and when it was written. A brief account will suffice here. The thirty-nine Old Testament books are not printed in the order they were written down. The earliest Genesis account of the Creation was written about 1000 BC (the time of King David) and the story, with the later strands that had been added to it, was finally edited about 400 BC. So while the earliest stories, Adam and Eve, Noah's Ark, the tower of Babel are, quite correctly, read as the mythic prologue to Israel's history, they were written in the light of that history and the stories bear the imprints of a consciousness evolved at a far later period. Most of the Old Testament texts were put into their present form after a later (fifth-century) return from captivity (this time by the Babylonians). The kind of cohesiveness and moral seriousness we "read back" into earlier narratives derived most fully from these later experiences.

If we simply take the texts as they come it is very hard, for example, to square the Genesis command to man to "cleave to his wife" with the behaviour of the early patriarchs: those to whom God reveals his purposes. They were exemplary leavers of father, mother and homeland, but apart from Isaac they were not very good at cleaving! At this stage building up the community of Israel was clearly the paramount concern and this meant breeding male heirs. Jacob employed four mothers for this purpose, Leah, Rachel and their maids. Abraham two. Sometimes – as in the case of Abraham who lent out Sarai to save his own skin in Egypt – the survival of the covenant community simply meant staying alive at all costs.

Just as the seventh commandment clearly evolved, so apparently did the second if we take it to mean absolute transcendant monotheism. The nomadic stage of early Old Testament life was matched by faith in a supreme tribal god who reveals himself to a supreme tribal leader, the patriarch, and is closely identified with him. This god bears the name God of my father (Gen. 31:5, 29, 42 etc.). Each tribe had its own tribal god (which distinguished it from its polytheistic neighbours). The sequence of generations increases the number of these gods: hence terms like the god of Abraham, Isaac and Jacob were interchangeable with the term "god of our fathers" which came into usage when the tribes united. But god of our fathers is not the same as God the Father for it was only a later tradition which fused these deities into a single God and thus put explicit monotheism at the beginning of history.[6] Once we understand the evolving nature of both precepts then the cultural-religious background against which they evolved becomes crucial to our understanding of them.

Cultural studies reveal the social origins of male monotheism to lie in the nomadic, herding societies of the Middle East desert. The people's way of life itself "in that vast terrain where the vault of sky looms majestic and earth appears quiescent, bare of vegetation", gave power and resonance to an image of god as Sky Father. They were also intensely patriarchal and highly polygamous. The patriarchal chief would have had a "top wife" like Sarai and headed a clan of several hundred, consisting of several wives as well as slaves, concubines and all their children. When and as this community came to adapt itself to a more settled agrarian life this family structure shrinks from the loose confederation of the clan.

Wives and children could no longer be acquired and shed at will, since they became economically necessary. "Slave labour was for most people unavailable," writes Bertrand Russell, that great debunker of biblical morality, "and therefore the easiest way to acquire labourers was to breed them." And presumably keep them.

The Canaanites were an agrarian people, long settled in the lush Jordan valley with its finely built cities, cradle of one of the earliest civilizations. We know very little about their day-to-day marriage practice and it would be absurd to assume them to have perfected the practice of monogamy, but the patterns outlined above would suggest that they were more likely to be "advanced" in this respect, and to be shocked by the sexual habits of the invading desert tribesmen, than vice versa.

It goes without saying that this is not how the story is presented in Scripture. We see struggle in military terms as a battle for the rightful possession of the land which the Lord had given them. This involved unseating both the Canaanite rulers and their gods, chief of whom is Baal who gets a very bad press indeed. This is not surprising on two counts: one, that nomadic societies are everywhere characterized by an aggressive, hostile relationship to agricultural peoples and their gods. Two, that the story (like all history of struggle, as Marx reminds us) was recorded by the winners, and victorious colonial powers rarely admit to erasing a morally advanced religious culture. It is also the case that the moral depravity of the conquered by which the conquerors justify their brutality is most commonly depicted in sexual terms. C. B. de Mille and his ilk have continued this tradition – think of those countless images of bejewelled voluptuousness which have clustered round the "others", Canaanites, Egyptians, Philistines or whoever in the Bible epic. The Church continues it too in its own way. The biblical exclusion of women from altar and place of blessing continues to be defended on the grounds laid down in this period of struggle with the Canaanites. Any inclusion of women in religious rites would signify, we are told, a return to a "pagan" world of "fertility cults". I am not going to re-run this old argument here; I wish only to point out how many of our culture's perceptions are founded on the moral degeneracy of extra-biblical religion.

But we also know that the Hebrew people absorbed much of this culture. Thoughtful readers and teachers of the Bible have come to acknowledge the immense enrichment Hebrew spirituality gained from its assimilation of the "naturalistic" elements of Canaanite religion. To it we owe the lineaments of a Creation-centred theology; a concept of God as lord and lover of Creation as well as lord of a particular people's history. The present-day quest for ecological awareness has itself raised the question whether the sky god of biblical patriarchy can stand alone without the balancing effect of a more immanent merciful, Earth-cherishing mother.

To understand the political and cultic hostilities which brought about her obliteration we need to bring our imaginations to the "other side" – to stand as I was privileged to do recently on the archaeological site of Jericho, looking at the layers of its history beneath my feet, and beyond at the plain over which Joshua came with his conquering host, wondering how the confrontation was really experienced by both peoples. Who was this hated Baal, who has become a biblical byword for sexual decadence and pagan super-stition?

As Rosemary Ruether writes:

the ancient Near East world displayed its continuing attach-ment to the prehistoric myth of the female as the primary divine power upon which the male as king or God depends. The king as son and consort of the Goddess represents the powers of vegetation and rain threatened yearly by searing drought. In the Babylonian and Canaanite versions he is represented as defeated by the powers of death and drought and then rescued from the underworld by a powerful goddess who conquers the dark powers and raises her son–lover from the dead. The resurrection of the king culminates in his marriage to the Goddess who thereby elevates her human husband and places him on the throne. Renewed fertility and legitimate political power are thereby assured.[7]

Ruether emphasizes the need to bring a "mythopoetic mind" to the Old Testament narratives. She came herself to an apprehension of Baal as "a real god", who revealed the mystery of life which had broken through into the lives of the people. Baal gave them the key to the mystery of death and re-birth. *"And there was more to him than sex"* [italics mine]. Baal was not some promiscuous phallocrat, mastermind of orgiastic indulgences, but secondary to the goddess who was the real author and arbiter of creation.

Now this really does seem a more realistic and gentler way than the biblical one of acknowledging the realities of generation, human or agricultural. As I have said, we know little about the day-to-day social life or the ordinary marriage practice of the Canaanites, but a spiritual consciousness in which male humanity sees itself as dependent on female constancy as a gift and a blessing – which is precisely what aggressive patriarchy everywhere strove to excise – seems worth acknowledging in its sexual as well as its ecological dimensions. If such a world view had prevailed it would seem unlikely that we should have inherited a model of monogamy in which it is seen as a gift of good men to their dependant women but the other way round!

It is not surprising that feminists have chosen to lay some restorative stress on the matriarchy versus patriarchy element of the Canaanite conflict. After all for those of us previously untrained in biblical scholarship it comes as quite a surprise to discover that it was not Baal who presented the main problem; he was only secondary to his Goddess Queen and consort.

Whether or not the participants in the struggle saw it that way we cannot tell from the biblical narrative. But from what we do know it is not hard to see why the older Canaanite religion appealed so strongly to many Israelites. They had returned from years of slavery and desert to cultivate the Promised Land. Yahweh, in his fierce singularity, had brought them through their trials with fire and cloudy pillar but they must surely have asked themselves whether he could also be relied upon to come through with the milk and honey.

Yahweh simply replaced Baal as consort to the Great Mother in popular piety, which seems a reasonable solution but one which clearly would not work: religious identity *not* being an area in which sensible deals are struck. But there were further reasons which cannot be satisfactorily explained in any of the terms outlined here.

The Hebrew people do not anyway quite fit any of these anthropological patterns. They were a people who had made the transition several times over from nomadism to settlement and most peoples do it only once. Hebrew religious consciousness was shaped both by the desert and by a knowledge of and longing for a homeland. Most important of all, the desert "represents" something far more than an earlier, primitive stage of their development, it is seen as a crucible of the people's destiny, a place where God showed his face most fully and burnt a knowledge of himself into their hearts. At some point the Exodus community learnt an absolute transcendence: that while God reveals himself in and through Creation, he and he alone stands outside it. God's "otherness" becomes a theological absolute which forms the root of Old Testament spirituality and lies behind all its codes and rituals. These are instituted to express and reflect the "order of differentiation" established in Creation itself. That which threatens

15

the integrity of this order threatens a lapse into primeval chaos. Sexuality is clearly the one area of life where chaos and un-differentiation looms largest: a place where the boundaries between individual bodies dissolve.

The "sacred marriage" as celebrated in Canaanite rite gave great offence both in its human re-enactment of the drama of death, renewal and creation – which implies that the human community can make it all "happen" by re-enacting it in imitation of the divine – and in its celebration, by what was clearly explicit sexual activity, the merging of human and divine life and the ecstatic, irrational merging of humans with one another.

Many scholars believe that Israel's rejection of Canaanite fertility religion was an affirmation of Yahweh as neither male nor female: in other words the creator of sexuality is the Other who transcends it. But this not does mean that the Hebrew God placed himself "above" sexual representation altogether. Like Baal there was "more to" Yahweh than sex, but his cult was no less sexual than those he thundered against. The sacred marriage motif was not absolutely rejected but rather adopted in reverse. A new "marriage" was instituted: one in which the community itself was collectively imaged as the Bride/wife of the one Creator god. This jealous God will have no others before him nor is he the husband, lover of any woman but takes to himself a people for his beloved and begets a nation's destiny upon her. Fidelity between spouses becomes more than a prohibition against anarchic adultery; it becomes a sign of the covenant between God and humankind.

The Promise, though, has to confront history; a history of male ascendancy. In a patriarchal community this theoretically "neutral" teaching is expressed in highly patriarchal terms. The first sign of God's covenant is visited upon the male body of his people: with Abraham's circumcision God promises the land of Canaan to Abraham's seed, promises to be on their side for ever and ever. Sarai and her descendant sisters do not wrestle with angels in the desert night nor hear the word of God told on the mountain. She eavesdrops in the door of the tent or waits on the river with the flocks, the children and the impedimenta of the journey until he tells her His will. Feminist Bible scholars have catalogued and categorized the ways in which women's lives were simultaneously controlled and devalued and their role in history excised. Marriage is described in predominantly patriarchal terminology, "wife" being a comprehensive category that covers all women. Wives are endlessly said to be "given", "taken", "sent for" and quite frequently "captured", which makes fairly depressing reading. As do the Law's countless provisions for men's seemingly immutable need for more than one sexual partner.

The idea of God as tender faithful husband is not very persuasive in a culture where real life husbands conspicuously and outrageously fail to show forth the image of their maker. The sexual double-standard became enshrined in both Law and history.

It simply is not good enough to counter feminist feelings of anger and exclusion by telling us that God is not *really* male or by accentuating the positives of biblical marriage teaching. Judaeo–Christian women are called to locate their lives within the biblical framework and to shape their sexual behaviour according to its rules, largely without benefit, as I have said, of contextual *gnosis*. If the first is difficult then so is the second, for the rules are inextricably entwined with the gender images – positive for men, negative for women – that the Bible presents. It seems to me perfectly just for Sara Maitland, for example, to point out that "Father Abraham is, frankly, a real bastard" whose vices – one being living off Sarai's "immoral earnings" – are all "re-named virtue ... this is called patriarchy".[8] Maitland's vibrant, passionate re-telling of the story of Abraham's relations with his wife and

17

Hagar, mother of Ishmael, shows feminist anger to be instructive as well as irreverent for she points out dynamics of the text that have been hidden from our Sunday School eyes:

> Here we see, perhaps for the first time in recorded history, one of the classic devices used by men against women. Sarah the wife gets blamed but not punished. Hagar the mistress gets punished but not blamed. Abraham gets neither, he has his cake and eats it too. This is neat.[9]

It is sobering to reflect just how much of the Bible's sexual instruction is either presented or interpreted in a woman-blaming context.

One early example comes in a passage of Genesis (6:1-4), the place where a subversive plurality of gods most explicitly invades the narrative. This is a dark and troubled tale of rape of "the daughters of men" by the "sons of God", leading to the birth of monsters. My Bible teacher's handbook comments that this piece of "pagan mythology" is included to illustrate "the evil that infects not only men but even celestial beings. It points to a cosmic dimension to evil which more than justifies the judgement to come."[10] This judgement was underscored in Scripture by placing the story as prologue and pretext to Noah's Flood. Significantly, later patristic tradition was to change the "rape" to "seduction", marking these "daughters of men" as dangerous sexual temptresses. It is in the intersecting processes of biblical-ordering-of-texts and patriarchal interpretation that feminist theologians have discerned the anti-woman bias of the entire tradition. The above story provides an early example of how blasphemous promiscuity came to be identified with femaleness.

Soon after this we meet the next famous "couple" of biblical mythology, Noah and his wife, central figures of the second Fall and rescue of mankind. While Adam and Eve were (more or less) equally complicit and played equal roles in the first

Fall drama, we have a totally different picture in the second. The human family is preserved by Noah's virtue and resourcefulness. Mrs Noah, unnamed along with her "sons' wives" is the first of a long line of "mates" who trundled behind Man. They were all loaded, with the beasts and the baggage on to the Ark which bore the entire created order from the borders of myth to "real" history. Noah's "rule over" his wife seems complete here since it is not described as part of God's curse but rather assumed, along with her silence and passivity, as part of his purpose. Of Mrs Noah's "desire" we know nothing. She does not, however, entirely escape blame in Christian tradition: the medieval playwrights tell us that she only went along under protest, preferring to stay with her women companions. But there was no turning back for her, for Mrs Lot or any of their descendant sisters.

The idea of conjugal fidelity as an image of God's love and care appears only fragmentarily in early Hebrew consciousness. Only once, in Hosea, does it become a central theme. Hosea records another tale of wickedness and judgement, set this time in the "real" history of the eighth century BC. At this stage Israel's political hopes had collapsed; the Kingdom was divided and the danger of invasion (by the Assyrians) loomed ever larger. In an extraordinary amalgam of symbolic and biographical narrative, the prophet Hosea tells the people that this is God's judgement on their spiritual "whoredom". He records God's command to live out the drama in his own life by taking "a wife of harlotry" to show that Israel itself had committed great harlotry in departing from the Lord. Hosea "went and took Gomer the daughter of Diblaim". We are told that after her marriage to Hosea, Gomer left her husband and fell into slavery of some kind. Hosea rescued her, paid her bond price, forgave her and made her his wife again. The story shows that, just as Hosea could still love his faithless wife, so God himself could be depended on never to give up his fierce love for the wayward Israel: "And I said unto her, Thou shalt abide with me many days; thou shalt not play the harlot, and thou shalt not be for another man: so will I also be for thee". (Hos. 3:3).

Hosea and the prophetic tradition he represents mark a new stage in biblical thought. The prophets reject the old "magical" view of God which seeks to appease him by sacrifice and ritual. Expiation by these means was still allowed, but God's favour is only guaranteed for those who made proper amends, material amends from their wrong doing. Canaanite religion stands under the judgment of this new ethical rigour but so also, and even more adamantly, does Israel herself when she sought to reduce her own God to a guarantor of national and cultic supremacy. Hosea's primary concern lay with the social inequalities that had arisen under political power and prosperity. Here, in their neglect of the justice and righteousness demanded by God, lay their forsakenness by him. Hosea's powerful prophecy enabled the people to see their political misfortunes in a new light: as a punishment which was deserved and had to be endured but which also provides an opportunity for a new beginning.

In a narrative of haunting lyrical power we see again just how central is the desert experience to Israel's true identity. The prophet reminds the people that it was in the desert, when survival itself was in jeopardy, that they learnt of God's immanent presence and their own destiny. Here in the desert the woman, the bride, chastened and penitent, is restored to her patriarchal Lord:

> Therefore, behold, I will allure her, and bring her into the wilderness, and speak comfortably unto her. And I will give her her vineyards from thence, and the valley of Achor for a door of hope: and she shall sing there, as in the days of her youth, and as in the day when she came up out of the land of Egypt. (Hos. 2: 14–15)

But we cannot properly recover the unique insights and transforming power of prophetic teaching without also acknowledging the dense web of ambiguity that lies in and around its sexual imagery: particularly when, as in Hosea, such imagery bears the whole burden of the narrative.

We know intellectually that Hosea is not just fulminating against sexual laxity, for sexual sin is a metaphor for something far more universal and momentous: nowhere moreover is whoredom suggested as a female sin. The people themselves have forsaken the Lord by whoring after the gods of profit and security. But the mixture itself of biography and symbolism is nevertheless an uneasy one, not least because Hosea, the man, images God and Gomer the faithless wife represents the sinful land and its people!

There is evidence for the theory that Gomer's harlotry and enslavement consisted in her active involvement in Canaanite fertility rites. Hosea's polemic against Baal/Anath witnesses to the continuing power of this old love over the people's imagination. In underlining his central message that only the One true God is the author and giver of real – that is, spiritual, ethical – life Hosea repeatedly and somewhat aggressively juxtaposes promiscuity and *in*fertility. Hosea is a very human figure and his writing also exhibits signs of a patriarchal impulse to devalue, even to deny the power of women in the life process. The old emnity is never far away and I think it is vital to see Hosea's text in the light of the important distinction Ruether applies to prophetic teaching: "(It) is valid primarily ... as self-critique. When it merely attacks other people's religion, Canaanite in the Old Testament, Judaism in the New, it does not speak with any great insight."[11]

Hosea does speak with profound political insight but the positive, hopeful elements of his message are, not surprisingly, more elusive to women. Most women feel somewhat ambivalent towards the desert past to which the male writers constantly recall us. The desert represents something rather different for women – a place where the harsher aspects of patriarchy (which historically include polygamy and a rigid double-standard) hold absolute sway; where women's contribution to religion and culture was minimal and where the feminine aspects of God were totally repressed. Men on the other hand have throughout history tended to nostalgia for the old tough days of struggle, when men were really men and women knew their place!

Against the image of the forgiven adulteress stands the less promising historical reality of a society in which adultery was punishable by death, for both parties – and not for what we would call "moral" reasons. The Law's prohibitions against adultery turned on the issues of property and authority – the adulterer robs the husband of his property and the unfaithful wife defiles her husband's honour by giving to another that which belongs to him.

However it is important to realize that Hosea was also witnessing to important ethical advances in sexual matters. By the eighth century monogamy was well on the way to becoming both the social norm and an increasingly important ideal – hence, of course, the relevance and resonance of Hosea's and other prophets' use of the marriage analogy.

Hosea's use of the harlot/prostitute image is a particularly ambiguous and difficult one. He was writing out of a social and ethical context in which prostitution was a common means of subsistence for women. There were in fact several categories of prostitute in the Old Testament but the distinction between the kind of harlotry Hosea is concerned with and the purely economic/occupational kind is not apparent in our language as it is in Hebrew. In the transition from universal polygamy the prostitute served as the poor man's substitute for the extra wives which were unavailable to him in settlement times. The prostitute who simply served men's sexual needs was a figure of shame but because her sexual activity did not essentially affect paternity rights and patriarchal family structures she was treated as religiously neutral, a mere social fact of life. Hosea used a word for harlotry/whoredom which is best translated as promiscuity, to play the whore, be an adulteress; a word with a specific moral value implying betrayal of an existing marital relationship. So while Hosea's teaching represents an important impulse to "de-neutralize" sexual activity and raise marital transgression into the realm of ethics, it does not embrace the category of the ordinary "functional" prostitute. Thus a whole group of women continued to exist outside the ethical structures of the covenant and beyond the parameters of prophetic protest.

The Old Testament scholar Phyllis Bird suggests that prostitution was actually "strengthened by the increasing institution of monogamous marriage". Under monogamy the prostitute assumed the function she still has today – a safety-valve for the preservation of the family. The fact that this remains an unknown, unresearched area of biblical history demonstrates just how invisible such women were, existing only as sexual functionaries, on the margins of society.

Sternness and judgement give way to more positive affirmation in later narratives. Counsels to sexual fidelity came to prevail in the later exhortations of the poets and prophets and were, appropriately, addressed to men: "rejoice with the wife of thy youth ... loving hind and pleasant roe; let her breasts satisfy thee at all times; and be thou ravished always with her love." (Prov. 5:18–19).

These admonitions are more often practical than lyrical, however. Three lines earlier man is crudely enjoined to "Drink waters out of thine own cistern" and not let his own fountain flow for others! Again, in Malachi, the unequivocal reminder that "the Lord hath been witness between thee and the wife of thy youth, against whom thou hast dealt treacherously: yet she is thy companion, and the wife of thy covenant" is accompanied by a reminder of the real reason why God made them one, "that he might seek a godly seed" (2: 14–15). Yet, as Phyllis Bird concludes, later writings did more than provide PR for monogamy, they "assume (as ideal) a high correspondence between love and marriage".[12]

The ideal is most famously represented by the Good Wife of Proverbs and the Beloved in the Song of Songs. I will focus on these two contrasting images, since they are the most readily invoked in answer to feminists' complaint of biblical silence and negativity about female sexuality, and so it is important to ask how "positive" or representative they actually are. The proverbial Good Wife, she whose "price is above rubies", is usually contrasted with the bad wife, a nagging, contentious creature (thus providing ample ammunition for misogyny). The former's sterling qualities are set out in a "day in the life of" account, which shows her to be a high-born woman, an able manager on whom her husband relies to bring peace and prosperity to his household and free him for the political activity by which "he is known at the gates, where he takes his place with the elders of the land". Though oft promoted to defend the dignity of housework, this woman is no housewife but rather an active overseer of a home-based industry (who wouldn't want a wife like that?). Nor is she a "super-mum" for her authority extends beyond her blood family to a whole complex network of clan and servants. She is indeed a formidable figure – so much so that the Book of Proverbs constructs a theological metaphor in which this type of Hebrew wife symbolizes God's own immanent Wisdom which rules and reconciles the universe. She stands as a pre-Christian version of the Holy Spirit , an immanent presence, with God from the beginning. As such she represents a great advance in scriptural images of women. But she is no "new Eve": the sexuality, the "desire" and curiosity of this idealized woman is excised. She is not seen as sexual at all except that her children are mentioned. She is a provider whose whole being and energy are directed towards doing her husband good, not to bringing him joy.

24

For sexual delight we turn to the Song of Songs, a celebration of erotic love as the most prized of God's gifts. The human body is depicted in rich sensual images from nature: of wheat, apples and wine, and the heady passion of the lovers is mingled with real tenderness. The love-making, initiated by the man and the woman in turn, is touching in its harmony and mutuality: "I found him who my soul loveth: I held him and would not let him go, until I had brought him into my mother's house, and into the chamber of her that conceived me" (3:4).

As Phyllis Bird comments "the woman is portrayed as seeking out her beloved in the very same language used by Proverbs to describe the aggressive enticements of the harlot – but with no hint of condemnation".[13] But this unique extraordinary text with its "depatriarchalizing" potential is neutered in other ways. Its very mutuality distances it from real life marriage in patriarchal society. It does not use marital terms and in no way implies them. The Church has never taken the poem as a marriage metaphor. In fact as we shall see in chapter 3, it has done the very opposite and used the poem to discredit physical love. The Song owes its (contended) place in the canon entirely to its allegorical quality – to the interpretation of Bride and lover as God and Israel.

In reality, then, these two images – the Good Wife and the Beloved – are never united anywhere in the whole Bible. We are split at the root – wife and mistress; "good" mothering woman and mysterious sexually-desired Beloved. This split resounds through our culture to this day, throughout the lives and writings of those who have shaped and influenced its values. Examples abound, ancient and modern. (To give but one instance I have just read that the great psychologist Jung had a woman companion/lover outside his marriage. To what extent should we attribute the post-biblical dualties – *animus/ anima* – by which he so sagely pronounces on male and female "roles" to his own personal need to split those dual, contradictory influences on his own eminently respectable life?)

The main problem, of course, with these and all other biblical texts is that nowhere do we find women's sexual fidelity – which they clearly practised to a far greater degree than men – raised as an analogy of divine love. And here we have to ask whether marital fidelity, as a characteristic of or a loving response to the divine, can be understood as such if it is never imaged by women.

We know very little of ordinary marriage in Old Testament times. The "feelings" biblical wives and husbands bore for one another are rarely revealed. There are touching, fleeting glimpses of conjugal devotion – Elkanah "loves" Hannah, mother of Samuel, we are told: he comforts her barrenness and defers to her wisdom; Jacob served seven years for the "love he bore" Rachel. Just as Abraham at the end laid Sarai to rest with honour and renown, we find that burial epitaphs of the ancient world witness to men's heartfelt thankfulness for the comfort and blessing of a beloved companion. A long life together must have been rare and though Lawrence Stone may well be right in his observation that married people "invested" little emotion in each other, some were clearly pleasantly surprised. However in a society where all marriages are arranged, compatibility must have been more a matter of luck than planning. By and large, moreover, amorous intensity – when we hear of it at all – is depicted as a very bad idea indeed, since such passion appears, for the most part, to be exclusively inspired by unsuitable women.

Again and again we find the monogamous ideal contradicted and undermined by the old "temptress" theme. Our biblical heroes and leaders were brought low, not by their tyranny or licentiousness but by their single-hearted passion for the alluring, dangerous outsider, Delilah, Jezebel. Women who are beautiful and beloved enough to get a starring role or their name in the programme are usually both blamed and punished. Those on the other hand who are humble and suitable are punished by invisibility!

Take the example of David, the Lord's anointed and another great father of the people. He was a notorious adulterer but only condemned as such when his passion threatened the cohesion of the male community. This occurred when his "theft" of Bathsheba was compounded by the murder of her husband, Uriah the Hittite, an officer in David's army. Earlier in his career David amassed a whole clutch of wives while dealing with a minor rebellion. Chief of these was Abigail, wife to the traitor Nabal, who had shown great independence of mind in circumventing her husband's folly. She was rewarded by David's making her his wife and we never hear of her again. "Have as many as you like but keep them in line and don't break ranks" would seem the overall message.

We are not, of course, required to venerate, certainly not to imitate the sexual morals of the kings and heroes; but it is interesting to note the degree to which wealth and power were – then as now – passports to sexual privilege.

The ordinary man's move, whether willing or grudging, ethically inspired or merely pragmatic, towards monogamy is a significant one. It was not, however, a peaceful progression. The three centuries between the time of Hosea and the time when the Bible appears in its present form were a period of instability, conquest and exile. The era (*c.* fifth century BC) after the Return from Babylon was characterized by an increased solemnity and cohesiveness in Hebrew life. This is thought by many scholars to be the time when monogamy became absolutely central in Law and in practice. The context in which this took place is not a happy one. The priesthood which now assumed the status and authority once invested in monarchy was zealously concerned with national purity and religious exclusivity. This cultic rigour is represented by Ezra, a priest and scribe who demanded that men put away the wives they married in exile. The xenophobia once applied to top people was now applied to all. It was a harsh and ugly business: the measures taken against foreign wives and against "foreign elements" generally were quite brutal and doubtless caused a good deal of human misery, to say nothing of the ethical contradiction implicit in requiring men to repudiate the women who had in many cases adopted their faith as well as thrown in their lot with them during their exile.

The whole concept and construct of the Law must be mentioned here, since by constantly expanding and developing from its Mosaic blueprint to meet changing circumstances it is an important reflector of ethical changes. The Law actually did more than uphold patriarchy: on occasion it challenged and mitigated the brutality of ends-justifying-means legalism of figures like Ezra. Against Ezra are posed the more open universalist teachings of Jeremiah, Jonah and Ruth. These writings show a more positive side of the Law. They show that the honour which must be accorded to the stranger and the sojourner was indeed a sacred and oft-honoured principle, central to Hebrew piety.

The Law's very specific restrictions on the barbarity of war are interesting and not unconnected to sexual theory and practice. The female captive, taken for pleasure as battle booty must, like other rape victims and debauched slaves, be treated as a wife. This may sound like a dubious and inadequate compensation but such a provision is none the less extraordinary – even unique – in the light of the callous exploitation that always and everywhere accompanies war.

I am not suggesting that women should be grateful for the "protections" of *any* male-dominated militaristic system, since it is such systems which made us helpless in the first place. Why indeed should we honour or remain attached to this particular patriarchal culture let alone strive to obey its precepts when they have so rarely worked in our favour. Why not just put it behind us as a bad memory? We are living at a time when more and more women are doing just that.

But not only that. Many women are moving beyond

rejection of the Bible's God and going over to his old enemy the Goddess. Though dispossessed She has never been entirely suppressed and has returned to symbolize the divine within women – and to exalt all that is female in the universe. In Her image women can break free from the dubious protection of the Godfather whose sexual "morality" is anyway no more than a sanctification of male power.

The question how we can usefully draw on the symbols of older woman-centred religions to humanize the patriarchal monotheism that displaced them has long been under discussion in feminist circles. (Critics of this enterprise usually point to the dearth of historical evidence for the existence of past "matriarchal Utopias". This criticism has failed to notice that most "goddess revivalists" are not seeking past Utopias but rather an imaginative engagement with suppressed traditions.) The Goddess cannot cure all our ills but she can serve as an authentic *aide-mémoire* of a time before women came to be seen as auxiliaries to men. The Great Goddess of Babylon, for example, as we read in the psalms addressed to her, is neither mother nor lover. She is a person of sovereign power like a queen or a great priestess who imaged the female half of the world. She was, however, overtaken by patriarchy and this, as has been said, occurred, albeit in different ways, the whole world over. She had already lost absolute power by the time of her Canaanite existence.

While it is vital to understand how and why she was demoted it is important first to grasp the universality of the happening itself. Most women in the post-patriarchal world have no time, resources or leisure to concern themselves with the lost glories of womanhood, or the means by which their more privileged sisters can escape the worst horrors of patriarchal domination. For them their relationships with men will shape their lives, for better or worse, and so the pursuit of sexual justice is more to the point than the pursuit of abstract sexual autonomy. In the laws I referred to earlier we see, however fragmentarily, rudimentarily and androcentrically envisaged, an impulse towards this justice, and it is on that basis that I and other feminists argue for a new synthesis between dominant and repressed traditions.

It is the Law and the prophets rather than its more promising poetry that keeps me attached, albeit critically, to the biblical narratives. As I have understood it, only the One God of the Bible speaks of justice as integral to faith and salvation. Only here is the older nature religions' creation/renewal drama promoted to the stage of history and the political process. Western consciousness and action, and increasingly that of the whole world, have been decisively shaped by the Hebrew take-over of Canaanite seasonal festivals.[14]

I am not arguing for the "inevitability of patriarchy", still less for the superiority of patriarchal monotheism, but rather pointing to that which was unique in its biblical development. The biblical sacred marriage is initiated to serve a cosmic justice and harmony which lies beyond the cyclical order of seasons, human birth and death. As Ruether points out, not all parts of the canonical Bible rises to the promise of prophetic faith. The prophets' denunciation of injustice and idolatry does not embrace all categories of injustice: it manifestly fails to address sexist oppression (or slavery) and for this reason its marital and sexual images are both unconvincing and frequently degrading to women. But the prophetic dialectic itself, the unique enduring legacy of Old Testament faith, provides a means whereby future generations can discern and denounce the evils that lie behind their own historical crises.

The Bible is the only faith text which actually criticizes itself. "Whoredom" is cried against those who "sell the needy for a pair of shoes" *and* against those who use the "solemn assemblies" of conventional religion to escape the real demands of the faith – justice for the oppressed. Thus while the Bible accords the greatest importance to sexual relations it also works to put sex in its "proper place" in the ethical scheme of things. If we attempt to screen out the political meaning of "whoredom", to sexually privatize biblical judgement, we find ourselves among those who are "sent empty away". No amount of conjugal virtue will save us from its judgements. Angela West once described the Bible as a "scandalous book (which) speaks to women precisely because it is *not* a set of instructions about how to get your private passport to heaven".[15]

It is not that there are no ethics, personal or social, in extrabiblical religions, but their primary stress is on the restoration of immanent harmony rather than the conversion of history. We cannot recover lost harmony by "going back to nature", whether in ritual or lifestyle experimentation. The "descent of woman", whether seen in terms of her enclosure in monogamy or not, is connected not just to social forms but to an entirely and irreversibly changed relationship between humanity and the cosmos itself. Few of us can bear to imagine a real return to a pre-technological world where we are entirely dependent on the distinctly unreliable blessings of nature. It is somehow dishonest to bask in an "ancient wisdom" that we have not created and whose hardships have not been our portion. The comfort and security of our Western privilege has been bought from centuries of rape and pillaging of the earth and its poorer peoples and this demands that we must do more than tune into "Mother" nature: we must seek just relationships with all creation, human and natural.

We also have to ask whether goddess religions were religions of the sisterhood we claim will "save the world" today. As Ruether points out, the Great Goddess of Babylon was no egalitarian. She made no common cause with the females among her own servants and her prayers most likely came from male lips. In her Canaanite existence she embodied the mystery and awe of motherhood, which as Rich says, served to endow all women with a respect conspicuously absent in the patriarchal religion which overtook Canaan. But again do we not demand something more? We want a society, a religious and ethical system, that gives honour to femaleness itself, not just to mothers. The Bible conspicuously fails to do this: we cannot escape the impression that here, perhaps more than anywhere else, women were only valued for their child-bearing function. But the greater respect attached to women through motherhood in the wider world was not strong enough to halt the steady march of patriarchy. Nor did it stand against the intersecting notions of "sexual possession" and "property ownership" from which, in Rich's words quoted earlier, "developed the institution of (monogamous marriage) now known".

The magic and awe that surrounded motherhood did not ultimately survive the discovery of paternity. It is absolutely clear to me as a feminist that this knowledge has been abused by men. They have exaggerated and exploited what is after all a very minimal contribution to the life process, to wrest power and glory from women as the bearers and nurturers of life. The language of the Bible reflects this in the crudest and most aggressive ways – all those "begats"! But I want to add that while knowledge of paternity is power – and has been abused as such – all knowledge is. That is what the biblical Fall is all about! It teaches us that primal innocence is lost, along with a world-view that invested the Mother with awe and magic. Knowledge is also truth, or can be, and the truth will set us free, or should do. Children do come from their fathers as well as their mothers, and through the agency of grace come to "belong" to God and society as well. But this post-Fall process cannot begin unless women give the father his fatherhood, which must involve to some degree at least her sexual fidelity. This, in the light of historical patriarchy, means "loving our enemy" – a crazy thing to do – rendering to him that which he has, historically, rarely rendered to us. But biblical faith requires just that. Men are not let off the hook: if we envisage redemption as liberation from sin we must name patriarchal domination as a primary sign and source of sin. Redemption requires, among other things, that men see female fidelity as a gift of women to men. It cannot be defended as a "natural" universal right. It is by and large irrelevant in "nature" anyway; very few animal species practise monogamy. Nor should it be bestowed as a consolation for the "womb envy" that some men tell us they suffer from. Such a condition, if it exists, needs healing, not appeasing. We cannot give the name "ethic" to a practice based on male neurosis.

And I do believe that biblical tradition to be more than that! The covenantal theology of the Old Testament is potentially affirmative of this gift relationship between the sexes. The metaphor of God's marriage to his people, which became foundational to later Pauline ecclesiology, militates against male-dominated, highly individualistic concepts of family: particularly the modern nuclear unit of today which Rich quite rightly condemns for its "supernaturalizing of the penis, its emotional, physical and material possessiveness."

In the end I have to confess that my attachment to the biblical narrative is instinctive and emotional. Its very warts-and-all familiarity gives me the freedom to impose my own imagination upon it. But there is in addition a strong element of personal preference. The Bible speaks in human rather than epic language and I like this roughness, this particularity. The themes of Fall and redemption highlight the tragedy of sexism for they help us to see Eve's plight as a sign and consequence of fallenness rather than an inevitability.

I am further persuaded to stick with the Eve version by looking at what happened to her outside the Bible. This chapter opened with the stories of Eve and Pandora. Both can be seen as demoted mother goddesses: Eve is actually named as "mother of all that lives". Pandora is the Allgiver, Allgiven; Eve on the other hand brings nothing to Adam but her curiosity and her woman's body from which she will, in suffering, bring forth life. For Pandora there is nowhere to go but down – she dwindles her way from Goddess to wifedom passively, sulkily.

By the fourth century BC, around the time when the biblical version of Eve was written and four centuries after the Pandora myth was recorded, the goddesses had become detached from their earlier political base and become the focus of personal devotions. In her Classical existence the Goddess is divided. She came, in varying combinations, to represent different "stages" or various – but all patriarchally perceived – "aspects" of womanhood: Maid, Wife/mother and Crone.

Many people, men as well as women, prefer Classical religious symbolism, not least because it gives us female divinities. There is more variety, more room for manoeuvre, as it were, in polytheistic systems. The existence of more than one God circumvents the knotty problem of "his" gender. There are also more accessible, varied and above all *humorous* ways of seeing our human sexual predicament. But I want a theology which unites womanhood, not one that splits us apart, and for that I will, reluctantly, give up the laughter. While I can happily "identify with" figures like Athena, wise and independent, I have to reckon with the fact that as, middle-aged married mother I am represented by Hera – a nagging, querulous, jealous creature. I find more dignity and hope in my Eve-image.

(Or perhaps not. To be honest, I sometimes prefer the fate of Lilith who in Hebrew mythology hovers menacingly around Eden. She was Adam's first wife, the first woman made by God in God's own image. Adam did not like her pride and insubordination and so asked God to give him another wife – made according to Adam's own specification. God, being obliging and believing in free will, did so and there we are. Waiting for Lilith, who mocks and challenges the "wife" in us, I find it significant that, for me, the most rebellious and

inspiring alternative to the patriarchal myth springs directly
from it and is somehow contained in it.)

As it is, life is rough for Eve. She gets her share of sweat
and those accursed thistles as well as Adam's rule. Their partnership was wrought, as Engels tells us, in sin and necessity,
in Eve's desire and submission and Adam's brutalization.
They are given a job to do, to rebuild the world in God's
image. Theirs is an ethical struggle – there is no turning back
from the knowledge of good and evil. But it is in the shame
and the struggle that the divine spark is lit in human hearts.
It is a beginning.

2

Scandalous Particularity:
New Testament and Early Christianity

By this grace dissolved in place. (T. S. Eliot, *Marina.* Ariel poems)

Have ye not read, that he which made them at the beginning made them male and female. And (he answered and) said, For this cause shall a man leave father and mother, and shall cleave to his wife: and they two shall be one flesh? Wherefore they are no more twain, but one flesh. What therefore God hath joined together, let not man put asunder. (Matt. 19: 4–6)

In this one teaching, recorded in all the Synoptic Gospels, Jesus upholds monogamy as the cornerstone of Judaeo–Christian sexual morality. In Matthew adultery is explicitly condemned as giving cause for divorce, which strikes against God's Law and purpose for humankind.[1]

There are few further recorded comments on sexual matters. Jesus pronounced no "new" sexual ethic and clearly rebuffed any suggestion that he should do so. He had come, he said, not to overturn the Law but to complete it; and that if we love him we will keep the Father's commandments. For all kinds of people Jesus' marriage teaching sets an impossibly high sexual standard: it has demonstrably brought about the most futile, crippling guilt in those of us who fail to reach it. Nowhere does Jesus modify this teaching. Indeed in the Sermon on the Mount he went even further, saying that "except your righteousness shall exceed the righteousness of the scribes and Pharisees, ye shall in no case enter into the kingdom of heaven" (Matt. 5:20); and when, in spelling out the ways in which the commandments should be exceeded,

he came to adultery the standard becomes even more impossible to meet: "But I say unto you, that whosoever looketh
on a woman to lust after her hath committed adultery with
her already in his heart" (Matt. 5:28).

The Gospel, then, would seem to give sparse comfort to
proponents of sexual permissiveness. The difficulty some Bible
moralists might have with combating adultery of the heart
has been summed up in a well-known cartoon in which one
monk says to another: "If it's as bad to think about it as
it is to do it, what on earth are we doing here?"

Those of us who oppose the direction the moralists' crusade
seems to be taking do so on rather more serious, solid grounds,
which will, hopefully, emerge in this chapter. While few would
wish to deny the seriousness of the sexual crisis they speak
of, diagnoses and their applications can vary dramatically.
However as a Christian I am positively required to look to
the Bible for guidance; Jesus promised that a reflection on
his words and the Scriptures will lead us to God who is All
Truth. I find it raises questions and concerns that many
traditional Bible moralists have failed to address; and that
these questions and crises were present in the society to which
Jesus himself ministered.

What then is "Bible morality"? Jesus spoke within and for
the Law of his own Hebrew faith where his contemporaries
were having some problems interpreting the Father's commandments. The question which elicited the "one flesh" statement was unmistakably a trick question, an attempt by a group
of rabbis to draw Jesus into a long legal wrangle over divorce
which had reached crisis proportions at the time of Jesus'
ministry. But before we come to that let us recall the actual
words and images used in the statement. I believe that while
the Church has enthusiastically promoted the precept Jesus
laid down it has failed to grasp its optimistic core. Jesus
affirmed one-flesh fidelity as a sign of Paradise Restored: it
was both command and promise. Man and woman are

restored to one another in Christ, "the image of the invisible God, the firstborn of all creation", through whom and for whom all in heaven and on earth are reconciled (Col. 1:15, 20).

The promise has been largely obscured by the androcentric anthropology within which all biblical teaching has been formulated. The influential teachers of the Church, up to the present day, have seen men's rule over women as "natural" and so have projected it backwards in time on to the original order of Creation to which Jesus was recalling us. The earthly fathers seem to have forgotten that Eve's desire, which "shall be all for a husband to rule over her", was instituted not in Eden but at the Fall! So long as the new Eve is anchored to the old order by this one thread the most elevated Christian morality will fail to reclaim the goodness and godliness of her "desire", her sexuality, for it is seen not in relation to God but to men. This is apostasy. It is absolutely clear to me that feminists' protests against the sexual objectification of women needs to be properly heard and incorporated into the present debate.

Feminism, along with other movements for social change, challenges the whole concept of "personal morality" as a separate category of ethics. "The personal is political," we say. Our sexuality is not a separate or neutral part of our existence; it embodies our whole being, and so the social, economic and cultural context in which we live out our "private" sexual relationships must be brought to bear on questions of sexual integrity. And vice versa.

Those of us who are Christian would see this approach to be validated in Jesus' teaching. He showed himself to be deeply aware of the sexual oppression women endured in contemporary society. He clearly recognized the overall patriarchal context in which the Law had developed and when asked his trick question specifically condemned the masculinist bias. Jesus described the old Mosaic divorce law as a concession to human fallenness. "Because of the hardness of your hearts," he said, Moses "suffered you to put away your wives; but from the beginning it was not so" (Matt. 19:8). "Your hearts" clearly meant men's hearts, whose hardness was manifest in a ubiquitous sexual double standard in women's status as property at the disposal of fathers, brothers and husbands. Women were never the beneficiaries of the divorce laws' concessions and their victimization had been greatly exacerbated by abuses that had arisen. (One faction in the rabbinical quarrel favoured an extremely "generous" interpretation of the Mosaic Law, by which any source of displeasure, even something as trivial as untidy hair, was reason for a man to dispose of an unwanted wife.) Here was a clear case for a righteousness exceeding the scribes and the Pharisees as well as an example of the importance of paying attention to the particular historical circumstances Jesus addressed.

His concern for sexual victimization is seen most clearly in his treatment of individual women. He was tender towards women's needs and particularly forgiving of their sins. It is from examples of his treatment of women sinners that we *know* that Jesus himself did not see sexual sin as beyond God's healing power. In his dealing with a woman taken in adultery Jesus sternly rejected the idea that her sin fell into some "first stone" category. "I tell you," he said of another woman, Mary Magdalene, who anointed him and washed his feet, "her sins which were many are forgiven because she loved much." Jesus' love, understanding and forgiveness in sexual matters was applied only to those who had been deeply wounded by society's hardness of heart. It cannot therefore be thought of as a comforting blanket to be laid over the harshness of the sexual standard he laid down. What is not often remarked on is that women provide not the best but the only examples of forgiveness of sexual sin in the Gospel narratives: there is no evidence that it was offered to the stonethrower, the whoremaster or the polygamous husband.

39

Gospel stories of women further contradict the idea, so often found in today's crusade, that sexual sin, though forgivable, automatically disqualifies the sinner from positions of leadership and spiritual authority in the churches. Jesus shared his own deepest thoughts about the nature of his ministry with the woman at the well, the woman he made "first apostle to the Samaritans".[2] She was a stranger and a foreigner who Jesus knew to have had five husbands and to be presently cohabiting out of wedlock. In this, his longest recorded conversation, Jesus is brought to concede the woman's prophetic arguments for redemption for the non-Jews. She met no disapproval or defensiveness in Jesus, only praise for her faith: a faith in which all are free to "go in peace and sin no more".

Conservative and radical alike recognize Christ's great love and respect for women. It is commonly said that in the love and respect he showed to women Jesus himself was ahead of his time. I want in this chapter to ask if and how this is true. How can this be reconciled with his terse uncompromisingly traditional stance on monogamy? Can this teaching really be "good news" for women and for society as a whole?

The fact that Jesus taught absolute monogamy in the context of sexual justice cannot alone win the day for Bible ethics. It can be argued that offering women greater protection in marriage serves only to mitigate not to challenge women's dependent status. Modern women who have achieved a degree of control over their lives are less and less likely to seek protection from males: they are more likely to question the whole basis of a society and a religious culture which makes such protection necessary. The circumstances under which prophetic assaults on male perfidy have arisen are not, as I suggested in chapter 1, auspicious ones for women.

The Christian Church today claims to have mitigated women's low standing in "the world" and this claim rests, to a great degree, on the dignity and protection afforded to women through its insistence on monogamous marriage. But it can be argued that sexist oppression was upheld, even intensified by Christianity. There is considerable evidence for the assertion that women actually fared better in the (Graeco–Roman) world of late antiquity than under the strict sexual code of biblical religion: a system which many historians have judged as specifically and fundamentally detrimental to women's development, and indeed to the advancement of society as a whole. We find, too, that monogamy is often the first part of the patriarchal luggage to be jettisoned, along with patriarchal religious forms themselves, when new class, gender and economic freedoms come within people's grasp.

Renewed calls to conjugal virtue are still issued in times of economic retrenchment and insecurity; times when there is increased pressure on women to stay in line in the interests of family cohesiveness. Throughout the 1980s we saw a renewed emphasis on the importance of the family. The Church's co-operation is specifically required in the promotion of monogamy on the grounds that the nuclear family incarnates the highest values of Christian civilization.

So it is vital to recognize that at the same time as he upheld a strict sexual morality Jesus refused to endorse the clan and family chauvinism we have come to associate with it. In fact he did the very opposite. When blood-kinship loyalty was pressed upon him he repudiated it. Looking on those who sat about him Jesus said, "My mother and my brethren are these which hear the word of God, and do it" (Luke 8:21). He went further and taught that "If any man come to me, and hate not his father, and mother, and wife, and children, and brethren, and sisters ... he cannot be my disciple" (Luke 14:26). The first Christian disciples left home and hearth to follow a master who offered them an entirely new kind of family; a beloved community of equals. This community, this "household of the faith" (Gal. 6:10) is now the base metal from which the new order is forged into being. Married and family love is contingent on this new community; fine if it serves the Gospel, but we are enjoined to remember (Luke 14:20) that a family wedding is no excuse for missing the real Family banquet!

A bourgeois church preaching the nuclear family as the foundation of the *civitas dei* – as Mrs Thatcher did with her now famous statement that "there is no such thing as society, there are only individual men and women and there are families" – not only insults those people who do not live in the nuclear set-up, it totally reverses this vital New Testament understanding.

Jesus was most startlingly "ahead of his time" in that he did not see women primarily as wives and mothers. He repudiated the old idea that women were blessed and saved through childbearing. When hearing the words "Blessed is the womb that bare thee and the breasts that gave thee suck", Jesus replied "No, blessed rather is she who hears my words and keeps them" (Luke 11:27–28). And her desire shall be for truth and self-knowledge and *not* "all for a husband" to rule over her.

Good news indeed when we remember that traditional morality and the pro-family package does little for those women who find themselves unmarriageable in a society which offers women security and subsistence only through marriage. Throughout history many poor and unprotected women had no choice but to resort to prostitution; the ultimate slavery for women but one which has been tolerated in Christian society as a necessary, albeit despised "safety-valve". It is no coincidence that St Augustine who wrote "remove prostitution from human affairs and you will unsettle everything because of lust", also regretted that stories of sinful women sullied the Gospel narrative!

When it has not denied it, the Church has tended to sentimentalize Jesus' loving companionship with "women of the town". Jesus did not, of course, tolerate prostitution: these

42

scandalous women were told to "go in peace and sin no more". But how, we may ask, in that society? She could neither "get a job" nor get "the love of a good man" and unless Jesus actually envisaged a society in which such women could live meaningful, forgiven lives then I for one would dismiss Christian sex ethics as cruel, contradictory pie-in-the-sky.

Jesus was not just "good with" such women, they were among his closest companions. Conservatives further obscure the respect for women that marked Jesus' whole mission by reminding us that, though "good with women" Jesus "only chose men" for the Twelve. It would be wrong to deny the theological and historical importance of the Twelve apostles. The post-resurrection vote to replace Judas shows the Jesus Movement's concern to observe a powerful numerological symbol of Messianic faith. But it is not uncommon, even among reasonably informed Christians, to confuse the terms apostle and disciple – I have often heard it stated that Jesus only chose men *disciples*, which is to deny the very real, active female involvement in the Jesus Movement. Victims of sexual injustice, then, must be not simply the recipients of forgiveness but are among those who will herald the new order, the kingdom in which all unjust relations are dissolved.

All of which brings us to the thorny question of Jesus' own political stance. What guidelines did he lay down for constructing the new order? Was he a first century socialist/ feminist? A social Utopian? A zealot freedom fighter? Or was his kingdom truly "not of this world"? The new faith–family of friends he inaugurated is rarely considered as key evidence in this debate. Or, when it is considered, it is used to suggest Jesus' disinvolvement with subversive social ideas and explicit resistance movements. Jesus' own itinerant lifestyle is seen as evidence of his otherworldliness rather than as a model of discipleship, which is, perhaps, not surprising in the light of Christianity's failure to sustain the new vision of family for any length of time.

This separation of medium from "message" is misleading, for the place of women and the function of the family and the household were neither private nor neutral issues in first century religion and politics. In both Jewish and Graeco–Roman life, blood kinship solidarity formed the lynchpin of the entire social order. By claiming absolute priority in the lives of its followers, the Gospel subverted converts' commitment to their own family. This family – which Jesus told us to "hate" – was not just a social unit, it was a religious unit united around its household ancestral gods. The family religion, in turn, tied the household to the public order or the state by representing a joint household religion which linked all the families together.[3]

As we have seen, Jesus rigorously upheld monogamy as a religious and ethical entity. But cannot we reasonably claim that he subverted its prevailing *function* of social control? By minimalizing Jesus' subversive stance towards the traditional family it has been far easier – and convenient – for the churches to preach a "private" morality which upholds state and family values and keeps Jesus' repudiaton of all systems of domination at a safe distance.

One of the ways this separation of private and public values is upheld is by restricting Jesus' iconoclasm to his relations with his own synagogue community. We are told, for example, that his unorthodox treatment of women – which he showed most famously when he affirmed Mary of Bethany's non-kitchen choice as "the better part"; and again when Mary Magdalene, first witness of the Resurrection, was commissioned to "go and tell" – offended "the Jews". This is no doubt the case (it was said that a man who taught his daughter the Torah "taught her lasciviousness" and women were not regarded as competent legal witnesses), but not the whole case. We cannot go on to assume that Jesus' message was only troublesome to "the Jews" or that their society was more rigid and backward-looking than others of the time.

Judith Plaskow, a Jewish feminist scholar, warns Christian feminists that their case against religious sexism often "depends on an extremely negative depiction of (Jesus') Jewish background, because the only way to depict him as a radical – that is as overthrowing tradition – is to depict the tradition as negatively as possible".[4] This warning should be taken seriously by all biblical thinkers for to take such a "short cut" to a feminist or any other Christianity is not only historically unsound; it perpetuates a pernicious history of Christian anti-Semitism, which is nothing less than a betrayal of Christ himself who "came to his own" and challenged and criticized them all the more because they were his own.

Another way, much favoured by liberals, of dealing with the impossibly high standard Jesus set is to point out that he spoke not as a legislator but as a prophet who is revealing a new theological dimension of marriage. I would myself argue for placing marriage in the context of the struggle between the divine promise and human hardness of heart. But it is unhistorical and unhelpful to speak of law and prophecy as opposites – one static, the other dynamic. I see Jesus not so much laying down "new" guidelines but picking up old ones which had been developed within the whole context of Old Testament faith. In both word and deed Jesus endorses a universal rejection of polygamy in favour of monogamous marriage. As I suggested in chapter 1, there are strong arguments for seeing this impulse as a progressive force, for, despite the patriarchal context in which it was developed, the biblical writers pressed for an ideal of mutual love and faithfulness between spouses.

How did this impulse unfold in Christian thought about sexual relationships? It is my conviction in writing this book that two fundamental conditions are necessary if humans are to conceive and practise an eroticism that is ethical, just, joyous and life-enhancing. Firstly, sexuality itself must be seen as a site of spiritual *and* social values; secondly it cannot be "compulsory", that is, celibacy must be genuinely honoured and available to both sexes. The choice whether to marry at all is clearly a basic human right as well as a pre-condition of any sexual ethic worthy of the name.

In her scholarly reconstruction of Christian origins, *In Memory of Her*, Elisabeth Schlussler Fiorenza traces the renewal movements in late-biblical Judaism and shows that:

> Judaism had elements of a critical impulse that came to the fore in the vision and ministry of Jesus. The reconstruction of the Jesus movement as the discipleship of equals is historically plausible only in so far as such critical elements are thinkable within the context of Jewish life and faith. The praxis and vision of Jesus and his movement is best understood as an inner-Jewish renewal movement that presented an alternative option to the dominant patriarchal structures.[5]

We know that Jewish thought took the first condition very seriously indeed. We do not, however, readily associate it with the second. Closely connected to the stereotype of Jewish patriarchal rigidity is the ostensibly more favourable one of their robust, unambiguous appreciation of sex and fertility. So much so that celibacy would be an unthinkable pursuit. If this was the case then Jesus' life-style and his seeming refusal to absolutize prevailing family forms would have been a purely oppositional "alternative". But such was not the case.

Alternative forms of community had become well established in the sectarian forms of Judaism, which were, as Ruether points out, *"the immediate roots of Christianity* [italics mine] ... central to the interpretation of the earliest Christian world-view as found in the New Testament itself".[6] These communities were largely founded on ascetic teachings, which will be looked at in more detail in chapter 3. However I should stress here that a sharp differentiation between married and celibate practice was not a marked feature of early New Testament life but a development of later Christianity.

It was the counter-cultural ideas that flowed around both Jewish asceticism and the new concept of family proclaimed by the Jesus Movement that proved troublesome to the powers that be.

The faith was born in a corner of the world where Greek culture and Roman order reigned supreme. In its early days Christianity was correctly seen as a variation of Judaism, therefore a Jewish "problem". The Roman masters had no great problem with the idea of Jesus' divinity: in fact they were rather surprised that the Jews minded this claim so much. The Jews were well known for being "different", a seditious, stiff-necked people with their odd ideas of historical destiny and their tendency to produce troublesome prophets; but in so far as they were a racial as much as a religious body – in so far as you could not "become a Jew" and Jews did not proselytize – the difference could be tolerated.

You could, however, become a Christian; and Christianity made its claim on individuals regardless of family or nation. It also declared all other religions to be false. The Christians were dedicated propagandists whose declared aim was to win the world to Christ: Christ the Jew, the fulfilment of Jewish hope. It was when they began to succeed in this aim "adding daily to such as would be saved", that the faith, root and branch, came under scrutiny: the social nuisance value of its teachings became clearer and persecution began.

The question now shifts from whether Jesus was ahead of his own culture's time to the threat his teachings posed to the wider world. To understand the conflict between Christianity and the Roman masters in all its dimensions we would need to know more about sex and family patterns in this wider world and their connection to religious observance. This is not easy; the most accomplished and painstaking scholars do not pretend to have arrived at an authoritative picture. As

Peter Brown has noted in his important new work on early Christianity, *The Body and Society*, "stereotypes, alternatively placid and histrionic, gravitate round (this period) with remarkable ease".[7] The old idea that Bible folk stood against the moral corruption of the ancient world continues – on celluloid depictions of New Testament life with decadent, tyrannical Romans replacing the Philistines or whoever, and in popular evangelism. These images bear little relation to reality and it is altogether more helpful to stress the similarities rather than the differences in sexual practice. The patriarchal family, the sexual double standard that undergirded Jewish sexual mores, was present in Graeco–Roman culture too. There is no question that the Jewish/Christian sexual strictness presented problems *per se*. The Roman masters were themselves rather moralistic in sexual matters; strong on "family values" and hostile to deviant sexual behaviour. It cannot be too strongly emphasized that monogamous marriage had long been the norm by AD 1, instituted in fact by the polytheistic Greeks long before the monotheistic Hebrews caught on to the idea. The Romans also gave the highest value to marital concord and affection between spouses.

Under colonial domination monogamy takes on a particular social importance. The strong patriarchal family and "good" women's enclosure within it provide the time-honoured consolation of strict home rule for male society humbled by the conqueror's yoke. It is even more essential for the rulers themselves who need to maintain a docile, well-ordered subject population as well as the social cohesion of their own.

Jewish Christians became suspect when they did not take their own family values seriously enough, though this could be seen as evidence of their backwardness. But as Christianity gained converts among the pagan peoples governed by Rome it threatened to dislodge the lynchpin which held Roman order together.

Persecution came insidiously at first by rumour and discreet gathering of information by the Roman authorities, followed by periods of close surveillance of daily domestic life in Christian households. The Imperial paranoia that flared up in waves of persecution in the first three centuries AD was rooted in the fear that Christianity subverted the social order, not just in its public political form but in its most intimate base in the family.[8]

The little we do know about family life in first-Century Rome is entirely drawn from the upper echelons of Imperial society. The civic and religious values of these people were based on a sophisticated understanding of the human body and its place in the scheme of things: "The family and the city determined...the body's connection with the natural world." Such tolerance as there was extended to extra-marital sex – a tolerance which, as Brown comments, immediately strikes a modern reader "as marked by a graciousness and a matter-of-factness that vanished in ... the Catholic West" – was based on a sense that the antithesis to the animal world, the city, was so strong that, once made, the claims of the city were inexorable."[9]

Not so for the Christians, as far as we can tell from the record of Acts. The apostle Paul hammered home the defiant message that the body was nothing less than the temple of the Holy Spirit; it belonged not to the city but to the Lord. As he did so it soon emerged that the primary threat posed by the Christian Church to the present form of the world was rooted in ideas of the human body itself. The Classical consensus was based on what Brown calls "benevolent dualism", a belief that "the soul met the body as the inferior 'other' to the self".[10]

Dualism is a word that looms large in religious and ethical discourse, particularly in the field of sexuality, and so needs some definition here. It means splitting Creation itself, and the means whereby we perceive it and interact with it, into

C

divisions of higher and lower. The dualism that became prevalent in Classical thought by the first century AD is commonly called spiritualistic dualism. Plato and his followers saw the human soul as timeless, changeless and immaterial, set far above bodily senses which were seen as of no account in knowing the real world. The wise man is one who keeps the body in its proper place because the ultimate aim of his existence is to transcend bodily experience and live in the realm of pure contemplation.

Though the Christian world inevitably succumbed to dualistic thinking – it was impossible to resist, as it underpinned the language and thinking of those cultures into which the Church sought entry, as we shall see in later chapters – it was and remains a heresy, one to which much of the negativity in Christian sexual thought can be traced. It has however become a catch-all word and it is common to explain away *all* the wrong turnings Christianity has taken by attributing them to "outside influences" rather than the universal human propensity to sin!

Dualism clearly offers great consolation in a world where death, pain and corruption stalk around – a function we can safely despise today, but for those who lived then it must have made life infinitely more bearable. It was not, however, benevolent when applied to the rest of the world. As Sara Maitland points out:

Dualism is a fundamental *ground* of oppression – the ability to assert that me and mine are better than that which is Other, and justifying this by making God the ultimate other, over in one's own image. It is worth noting that people do not create dualistic systems which put themselves or their own group at the bottom of the division. Dualism means the emotional and intellectual justification of élitism: theoretically that need not be true, historically it has always been so.[11]

The body becomes for those who can hope to transcend it – which those at the bottom of the social pile clearly cannot – despised and intractable matter "as intractable as women, slaves and the opaque and restless populace of the cities," whose existence was mediated by the city's rulers. The Christian communities which began to spring up all over the Empire were made up of slaves and ex-slaves who had precious little opportunity to transcend bodily existence, even if they were so minded.

Spiritualistic dualism did not lead the average noble Roman – as it was to lead later Christians – to shun sexuality. Marriage and procreation remained a duty, as the Emperor Augustus once sternly reminded Rome's bachelors. But once the body itself is getting a bad press then that which is most actively and visibly involved with its production gets a bad press too, that is, the sex act, and women themselves. Spiritualistic dualism thus becomes inextricably intertwined with what we call sexist dualism, a perception of women as inferior, closer to nature and all that a civilized man wishes to keep in its proper place. The first will *always* lead to the second; but not automatically the other way round. The operation of dualistic ideas will clearly depend upon how the spiritual – the ultimate Other – is conceived.

The Lord God of Israel is One God. I believe it is this central precept of monotheism that made for a considerable degree of Jewish resistance to the spiritual dualism that gained increasing ground in Classical thought. Mind/soul over matter cannot gain credibility when God is in all these things. In Jewish tradition God is revealed not through the "pure contemplation" of abstracts but in history and Creation. The incarnation of Christ, fully human and divine, reaffirmed the goodness of earthly existence. Human sexuality serves God's work of Creation and God loves everything God makes. At the heart of its teaching lay the Christian insistence on the value of the individual, the sanctity of daily bodily life itself.

This clearly did not serve the proper purpose of religion, which was to soften the blows and brutalities of everyday life, but rather challenged the passivity with which most were required to live in the closed and rigid society of Imperial Rome.

I must make clear that I do not believe my Judaeo–Christian forebears were automatically more holy or righteous than their contemporaries. Hebrew society shows all the signs of acute sexist dualism – as Jesus' own teachings make clear. In terms of "civil rights for women" they can be argued to have lagged behind the rest of the world. But these sins were not granted the same spiritual reinforcement that polytheism offered. A Roman could sit lightly to the "things of Venus" for she was only one rather lightweight divinity among many others. Sex and marriage might continue to present occasions of great sin for Judaeo–Christians, as we shall see, but they could not be divorced from the ultimate and weighty reality we call God.

As a feminist I see the full valuing of women as essential for the justice which must mark the integrity of the body. Here again monotheistic faith seems crucial as the spiritual basis of morality. The One God cannot ultimately be made over in the image of maleness, or, at least, there is a generic bluff to call when "he" is. As James Nelson puts it, "Israel refrained from absolutizing its patriarchal life as a theological assertion". As I see it, only Hebraic thought – of all the world-views of late antiquity – could expand towards an integrated ethical understanding of sexuality. Only the new family, the beloved community, proposed and lived out in the Jesus Movement, a family based on and not set above the community itself as the body of God, envisages a marriage practice which serves this body.

In the spring of AD 54 the missionary apostle Paul received a series of anxious letters from his supporters in Corinth. Scandal and division had arisen among them; a scandal so serious that it threatened to tear the new Christian body apart. In Paul's answer, set out in the first Letter of Paul to the Corinthians, he spelt out the major part of his entire teaching on sexuality.

Jesus had reinforced the Old Testament teaching, one God, one wife. Paul did rather more: he raised marriage from a sign of the covenant to an estate which signifies the mystical union that is betwixt Christ and his Church. If, as the *Encyclopaedia Britannica* states, "Christianity has had no greater practical effect on the life of mankind than in its belief that marriage is no mere civil contract, but a vow in the sight of God binding the parties by obligations of conscience above and beyond those of civil law", we have Paul to thank (or curse). An extended, elevated theology of marriage was the last thing on the minds of the people Paul addressed! They were rather wondering what part, if any, marriage was to play in the life of the new body. More immediately they were worried about "such fornication" even incest "as is not so much as named among the Gentiles" (1 Cor. 5:1).

Corinth, a thriving commercial centre close to a sea-port had, as such places are prone to do, become a byword for immorality to the travellers who visited it. It was, in Brown's words, a "sociological bear-garden"; full of people uprooted from their own culture by repeated miltary conquest, first by the Greeks and then by the Romans. About one-third of the city's population had been "imported" as slaves, as were the majority of those who formed the Christian community. A climate of moral and religious uncertainty prevailed in which, as Angela West writes:

> various sects and philosopher gurus were touting their particular recipe for salvation and the good life. Quite a few Gentiles were attracted by Judaism, with its monotheism and strong moral discipline and religious certainty . . . others were attracted by one or other of the many

mystery cults that abounded in the Empire at that time, where freedom was presented as the initiation into the knowledge of higher mysteries. Possession of such knowledge in some senses compensated people for the many material and political frustrations they experienced. The missionary movement of Christianity must have seemed to many to combine the benefits of both these salvation options.[12]

For Paul there was only one option – to be gathered into the household of Israel.

We cannot really know just how widespread was this notorious burst of fornication referred to above. We do know, however, by looking closely at Paul's reply, that it was more than an isolated, mindless lapse into hedonism. It was one of two extremes which had arisen from an explosion of the Spirit whose shock waves were felt throughout the young churches in those early days. This "first knowledge of the Church"[13] was an experience of the miraculous power of Love itself made manifest in ecstatic experiences of all kinds, prophetic inspiration, speaking in tongues, supernatural healing. In the belief that all was made new in Christ the Corinthians saw no reason why their newly founded community should replicate within itself the patterns of a corrupt society founded on property and slavery – or marriage, which could reasonably be seen as connected to both.

Sexual ecstasy was, in the minds of some Corinthians, inseparable from the new state of being wrought by Christ. Love not Law was the road to union with him, they proclaimed, and the right to seek out, and grow from, such ecstatic experience was part of "the glorious liberty of the children of God" (which the Corinthians, incidentally, also enjoyed in the sense of freedom from the persecution other communities experienced). This same blinding revelation led others to

a high-minded austerity which shunned sexual relations altogether in and out of marriage.

A common factor of both extremes was a fervent belief
that the Spirit cut across the old divisions of class, gender
and property. They were eager to embrace the new "commonism" described in Acts 2:44–46, where "all that believed were
together and had all things common; and they sold their pos-
sessions and goods, and parted them to all men as every man
had need". It is entirely understandable that for some the
marriage bond was seen as an irrelevance if not a hindrance
to this new life in Christ.

Of course both extremes – austerity and licentiousness, no
sex at all or "anything goes" – clearly undermine the old
ethic of monogamy, both in its symbolic base, which Jesus
affirmed, and in its social function, which seemingly, he did
not. How was Paul, who like Christ, envisioned the new life
not replacing but being "grafted on" to the old root, to check
this apparent breakdown of the old morality – a breakdown
for which he had every reason to blame himself?

Entry into the household of Israel was barred to pagans
by the requirement of circumcision and the Jews' food and
purity rules. As Peter had in the "test" case of Cornelius,
Paul too set these aside so that all could be one in Christ
Jesus in whom there was "no Jew nor Greek". The Corinthians
referred Paul to his own dictum that "all things are lawful
to me" which he had used when setting aside the Jewish food
rules. In Angela West's words:

this permissive phrase about the nature of Christian freedom seems to have boomeranged on Paul. For (one group)
have extended the logic of it and applied it to sex. The
gratification of sexual desire, they say, is like satisfying
hunger – a bodily function without spiritual significance
– so what is to stop someone gratifying this desire through
prostitution (*porneia*)?[14]

Paul had no quarrel with communal lifestyles and the sharing of goods. He had clearly grasped the new concept of family-as-beloved-community and was, throughout his entire mission, eager to build up the new churches upon this ideal. Paul had moreover reassured people that (some!) forms of Spirit-filled behaviour were the special marks of the saint.

But another notion altogether informed the sexual extremes: the idea that the physical body did not really matter very much anyway. This was very much a "mystery" cult belief, an expression of spiritualistic dualism which Paul knew well, being an educated man, a Greek as well as a Jew. Dualism was as often expressed in fastidious asceticism as in cynical permissiveness and we find both the ascetic and permissive "superspirituals" (as West terms them) receiving the full vigour of Paul's condemnation. They were, he told them, a precocious lot, "puffed up", self-important in their own spiritual wisdom. "Knowledge puffs up, love builds up", Paul tells them.

The "anything goes" version was of particular and urgent concern to Paul both because it was practised by people who sincerely believed they were applying Paul's own teaching and because it brought the community into disrepute.

Paul then is called upon to answer the age-old argument of "liberal" sexual permissiveness. Just how and why does sexual morality matter in such a unique and important way? Because it *is* "just" about bodies and the body itself has been claimed for Christ. Shun immorality, Paul tells them (1 Cor. 6:18), for "Every other sin which a man commits is outside the body: but the immoral man sins against his own body." As John Robinson has said, the concept of the body, *soma*, forms the keystone of Paul's theology:

It is from the body of sin and death that we are delivered; it is through the body of Christ on the cross that we are saved; it is in His body the Church that we are incorporated; it is by His body in the Eucharist that this community is sustained; it is in our new body that its new life has to be manifested; it is to a resurrection of this body to the likeness of His glorious body that we are destined.[15]

Sexual intercourse involves the whole body, not just its glands and organs: the whole person, heart and mind, and that whole person in community with others. Sex cannot be likened to eating, which is "just" a biological function – (even though one that can be transformed by table fellowship). Nor can sexual partners be seen as "goods" to be held in common.

Paul boldly, shockingly perhaps, takes up the Old Testament motif of "whoredom" when talking about individual Christians in the body of Christ. Sexual union with a prostitute – or anyone else – cannot be harmless, for casual sex cannot exist. "He who is joined to a harlot is joined to her for life", *henosis*. The sex act is irrevocable and indelible, so who you do it *with* matters. A "one night stand" is the equivalent of a pinch of incense on the altar of a pagan god – if it does not "mean anything" don't do it! Where you choose to put your body there your soul is.

These same truths are applied to the ascetic end of the super-spiritual spectrum: to those people who were asking Paul whether they should be thinking about sex at all; asking questions like, "should a Christian marry?" "Should husbands and wives abstain from sex?" "What about those yoked in marriage to unbelievers?" Paul is sympathetic to the idea that marriage can be a distraction from the great work now that, as was widely believed, "the present form of the world was passing away" and all contractual ties would soon be dissolved anyway. Celibacy or periodic abstinence can serve as a token of this future life, useful if it helps us focus upon God and the immanent kingdom. So, yes, it might well be better not to marry or, if widowed or separated, as Paul himself probably was, to remain as he is.

But Paul is tentative here and does not seek to dogmatize

this counsel. He, not the Lord speaks (1 Cor. 7:12), by permission and not of command (v 6). Nor does he idealize his own celibacy. He explains that his passion is not for spiritual freedom through celibacy but for the body of Christ of which we are all part, celibate or otherwise. Celibacy is not for everyone and cannot be seen as the "highest" calling – even though for Paul it is preferable.

The Corinthians and their predicament came most fully alive for me in the study (quoted above) which Angela West presented to a gathering of Christian feminists in 1982. She pointed out the startling resemblances between that community's turmoils and our own, as new converts (to feminism) *c.* AD 1970. The Christians at Corinth had found their liberation in this crucified and risen Jewish saviour who called them into a new fellowship of equals. Here was a source of certainty, of mutual support and growth denied them in the old world. But with feminism, as with the Jesus Movement, "the euphoria of unity in the new spirit did not last long before the cracks began to appear. In the 1980s we had to face the painful revelation that ... we are capable of being deeply divided on matters of sex" (as well as race and class). In the same way, Paul writing to the Corinthians in AD 60 is horrified, as some of them must have been, to find all the old conflicts reappearing right in the heart of the new body where they believed they were safe/saved from all that.[16]

It was illuminating to realize that the place of marriage in the new dispensation was also the burning issue for our Christian forebears in Corinth. Our own "1960s" legacy of permissiveness had, by the early 1980s, become the source of our moral confusion. It had not provided the freedom from Victorian hypocrisy and restraint that many had hoped from it. Nor had it abolished the old double-standard. Just whose sexual and social freedom had been promoted? Not women's, for sure. Does this mean that we are called, yet again, to seek "salvation" in traditional marriage? This would seem, for many of us, a denial of both our Christian and our feminist vocations.

West draws out a vital message for those of us in movements for social and sexual equality:

> Paul is attempting to show that salvation cannot in the last analysis be equated with gaining social or sexual freedom – with a shift in status from being married to not married, uncircumcised to circumcised, from being sexual to being celibate ... for however necessary it is to seek our freedom – and it *is* the heart of our Christian calling not to become "the slaves of men" and certainly our feminist one too! – yet that freedom cannot in the last analysis *depend* on the social or sexual freedom we have achieved. For that would mean that all those who had failed to achieve social or sexual freedom, for whatever reason, were necessarily excluded from any hope of being saved, safe.[17]

In other words Paul points us to the elitism which can often arise among people who have achieved a measure of choice in their lives. We can look on the lumpenproletariat whose lives are bound by necessity with the same benevolence – or scorn – as the pagan philosophers of old.

There were, of course, far fewer social or sexual freedoms and choices around in Paul's time. If we are to understand how Paul in his time envisaged sexual and social freedom and what he actually believed and taught about the nature of and place of marriage in the new order, we have to clear away some common misconceptions about the man himself. Some of these have arisen from Paul's own way of speaking about physical bodiliness. While he gives the highest value to the "body", both the word and the reality, he uses the word "flesh" in a very negative way indeed. In what Peter Brown has named Paul's "fateful 'theological abbreviation'", "the flesh" becomes the source of all temptation, standing for all that is opposed to the Spirit. This is one reason, among others, why so many people, in and out of the Church, cling to an image of Paul as a gifted and inspired missionary teacher marred by unfortunate hang-ups about sex in general and women in particular. Some even say that he contradicted the Lord's own will and words in these matters. This is of course absurd: we do not know if Jesus' own words were reported accurately in the Gospels, since they were written down many years after the event and some time after Paul's letter to the Corinthians. Paul never aspired to "interpretation" of Jesus' teaching. He saw himself, at best, as a pedagogue, a schoolmaster leading people to Christ. Above all he saw his relationship to Christ in terms of his own forgivenness: he sought to bring people out of the benighted state of sin he knew so well from his own past as persecutor of the faith.

The main source of Paul's bad press lies in the opening statement of 1 Corinthians 7: "It is good for a man not to touch a woman." This "proves" Paul guilty of both sexist and spiritualistic dualism, for is he not naming women as distracting temptresses and sexual contact itself as ungodly? But these are not Paul's words. He was quoting his correspondents' argument ("the things whereof ye wrote") prior to demolishing it. He was, moreover, talking to the ascetic not the permissive end of the superspiritual spectrum for he goes on to say, "because of *porneia*, let each man have his own wife, and let each woman have her own husband". We find that Paul is arguing for couples to get back to sex rather than away from it. His reasons may not seem very exalted but they are at least refreshing in the light of Christianity's history of tolerance of prostitution: the prostitute herself conveniently providing hygienic sexual release and set safely apart from the domestic sanctum.

Paul's other infamous phrase "better marry than burn" means just that. If sexual desire is an overwhelming distraction and celibacy impossibly difficult, then marriage – and he clearly means monogamous marriage – is the right way to deal with it. Paul's own lack of enthusiasm for marriage does not automatically presume a diminishment of its spiritual or socially "honourable estate" rather than an emphasis on the wider body of the community. This, not "individual men and women" and then "the family", is what really counts. Marriage is raised up from being a mandatory, primary institution into a vocation to which some, but not all, Christians are called.

And if we are so called Paul is clear that it is here in this one flesh that we participate in the body. Marriage too can stand as a sign that we are all members of one another, that "we are not our own". Paul's was the first Christian voice to claim a sacramental significance for ordinary married intercourse. We see, in Paul's advice to Christian spouses to stay with an unbelieving partner if possible, the importance he accorded the sexual bond through which, he believed, the unbelieving partner could be sanctified. For that partner becomes, by *henosis*, incorporated into the life of the new body anyway. This can hardly be called a negative, dismissive attitude to sex, though it may be an uncomfortable one!

Above all Paul stresses the importance of mutual consent in the sexual matters of which he is speaking. His counsel on the matter of periodic, occasional abstinence in marriage is striking in its egalitarian balance: "Let the husband render unto the wife her due benevolence and likewise also the wife unto the husband. The wife hath not power of her own body but the husband; and likewise also the husband hath not power of his own body but the wife." Paul does not assume, as many of his contemporaries and followers seem to, that the male partner is the one to define the relationship and make the important decisions. The old curse of Eve, in which female sexual desire and female subordination are shackled together, is dissolved here more explicitly, it seems to me, than anywhere else in Scripture.

We must remember, though, that Paul was a strategist as

well as the great "apostle of Love". In Paul's own lifetime he and his followers experienced the price paid by Christians for their new allegience – disrepute and death.

Paul is in a quandary here. His first concern is to build up the new body and nurture it. He is anxious to save the faithful from "worldly troubles" yet at the same time to keep them from being "conformed to the world". So he seeks, at various times and in various ways, to modify the conflict between faith and family; usually, as has been convincingly demonstrated by feminist biblical scholars, at the expense of women's freedom. But this concern should also be seen in the light of the ways Christianity actually took root and spread in the first-century world. It was a "grass roots" movement moving from the lowest ranks of society slowly up the social ladder. Those with the least investment in the status quo were the first to grasp the Good News while the more advantaged tended to cling to the privileges and safety of conformity. Until the fourth century AD it was still quite common for women, servants, daughters and younger male children to be Christians while heads of household and their heirs remained pagans. Home and hearth were vital field stations in the Pauline mission and Paul's advice to Christian partners to stay with an unbelieving spouse – far more likely to be a male spouse – if possible was also sound evangelistic policy. However Paul was not dogmatically anti-divorce. If the unbeliever wants out, so be it. We are called to peace, not strife, marital or other (Paul could, in this instance be said to have strayed from Jesus' own teaching, but on the permissive not the repressive side).

This historical context should be kept in mind when considering Paul's "household codes", those passages of the epistles where he urges wifely submission and modest behaviour. In any debate about women's place in Church and society, the Church – as well as those who wish to demonstrate the Church's oppressiveness – has chosen to remember and stress these passages rather than Paul's more radical statements in these matters. So it is all the more important that we remember that the codes were addressed not to "the Christian family" but to the divided household, where the real (spiritual) power resided in the women and other lower ranks. Paul's enthusiastic endorsement of women's leadership in the young churches seems to indicate that he was less interested in upholding the domestic status quo than many of his critics suppose.[18]

However, as we shall see in chapter 3, caution prevailed and the tentative compromises which Paul suggested have been hardened into theological absolutism. Paul's command to mutuality in marriage has been tidied away, filed under "Headship". Faithfulness in marriage, tamed into matronly conformity, loses all its subversive resonance as an image of God-love. As Charles Williams concludes:

(The Church) eventually lost any tradition of marriage as a way of the soul. This we have still to recover; it is, no doubt, practised in a million homes, but it can hardly be said to have been diagrammatized or taught by the authorities. Monogamy and meekness have been taught instead.[19]

Paul's teaching, when I took the trouble and the considerable help of Angela West and others, to explore it, has helped me detach my own practice of monogamy from the "meekness" our culture assigns to it.

Paul really does challenge so much of the conventional wisdom I grew up with. Back in the 1950s of my childhood, marriage was seen not, as it was for Paul, *a* way of knowing and being known in God but as *the* way for women particularly to seek security and salvation. Growing to maturity as a left-winger in the 1960s I was exposed to the opposite heresy we have considered here; a dismissiveness towards "personal morality". Sexual fidelity and exclusivity was dismissed as bourgeois possessiveness, stifling and trivial; a distraction from the greater need to "change society". No worse, I suppose, than the post-Pauline church's view of sex as a worldly distraction from higher, spiritual matters, but not much better.

In my own life I go all the way with what I call Paul's energy conservation policy – my translation of "better marry than burn"! Marriage really did release energies consumed by obsessively wondering who/how I loved and whether/when to marry. I fervently believe that for my partner and myself a sexually "open marriage" would militate against any real openness we try to seek with others in our life together. It would just mop up energy we need for other things that matter over, above and around our "private" relationship. I would hate to be for ever taking jealousy readings, tenderly checking on the feelings of insecurity and exclusion of the one in the outside corner of the triangle, which is what seems to happen to people who try to be "civilized and caring" in their practice of non-monogamy. It is the solemnity I find distasteful and I am encouraged to find that New Testament prohibition rests on the enslaving, distracting character of promiscuity rather than on legalistic considerations.

Sex is a powerful force, as we know, and Paul teaches us that it must be kept in its place, not because it is ungodly but because it is such a total experience that it can become too "spiritual" and all-consuming and only God can be loved totally. Alan Ecclestone, writing in the early 1970s for a Church perplexed by the recent "sexual revolution", says:

Somewhere without doubt the love of husband and wife and children is challenged by a still greater claim of God, somewhere beyond the "dull sublunary lovers' love" there is the supreme engagement of God with humankind ... it is the failure to see and work away at the connection between the immediate relationships we have with each other and our relation with God that goes far to retard our growth as people of God, so that we come unprepared to face the great question that God will put to us. Yes goes by default again and again because the occasions for learning how it is to be made have been lost in the sexual field.[20]

Women who have come to political and spiritual maturity through the challenges of feminism and modern permissiveness also find themselves instructed and liberated by Paul's down-to-earth pragmatic approach to sexual needs and conflicts. Janet Morley, for example, said in a talk on "Reclaiming chastity":

If we are to know God, then it is *in* the body and not out of it that we shall come to do so. That is why a deep sexual yearning for another person – the kind that turns you inside out – is not just an analogy for our longing for God, but a means of knowing it. *Similarly, the honouring of boundaries between us may also be a means of encountering God* [italics mine]. And yet the desire for God cannot be equated with bodily ecstasy; that is one kind of triumphalism. Nor can it be equated with detachment, or setting the body aside; that is another negative triumphalism. To be chaste seems to me, in this context, to involve challenging every kind of false solution to human sexuality. I suspect it will feel like a dialogue conducted over an abyss".[21]

Like the Corinthians we too live in a see-saw culture which veers schizophrenically between the two, and a pendulum choice of dualisms does not make for a vision of wholeness.

Chastity, taken in its traditional meaning to include fidelity in marriage, can, it seems to me, span the abyss. We can honour both the fierce exclusivity of the "Jealous God" and the God who calls us into openness and intimacy with one another with all the risks and real temptations that go along with this.

Yet our New Testament heritage seems to throw up more questions than it answers. Sex cannot become good and godly in a vacuum, only in relationship with a significant other. For all its potential of marriage as a "way of the soul" nowhere in the New Testament is the search for a soul-mate suggested as a proper concern for the Christian woman or man. For Paul "the appointed time" was too close, the conflict between faith and family too sharp for such refinements. When the idea of sexual "soul mates" finally came to cultural prominence (in twelfth century romance), it was not easily reconciled to the Christian sex ethic. It is hard to reconcile Jesus' "one flesh" promise or Paul's sacramental theology with the circumstances of marriage in the first century. It can engage our wills and our minds; we may approve, intellectually and politically, of a form of marriage which was firmly based in community interests not private whim, but it is hard for our hearts to follow. Arranged marriage, the norm throughout ancient society, remains anathema to many people. There is only one Great Love Story in the New Testament, "the supreme engagement of God with humankind". We do not know if conjugal sex was made more loving or conjugal companionship more cherished under its impact. For human love stories we go not to Scripture but to the rich storehouse of Classical mythology. Here are the stories by which we name our most passionate and perplexing experiences; here are the names we use to plumb the mysteries of the human psyche.

And we still live in and with the same contradictory influences of polytheistic, Classical symbols and monotheistic rigour which characterized the religious and ethical turmoils of late antiquity. We are the imaginative, intellectual heirs of Hellenistic thought which gave us, through the various Enlightenments of AD history, the sciences of the human mind, the multiple categories of rational thought which stand over and against the fleshly truths in which our Christian faith is so stubbornly rooted.

In the eyes of the world we are not people of sexual vision, we are the people of the book and the rules. Our rules seem to leave no room for the complexity of human sexual longing. "Being a Christian means holding your marriage together, doesn't it?" somebody said to me recently. A common if rather depressing view. But this is not the whole story. The rules have, for better or worse, formed the basis of Western morality and even when flouted hold considerable sway over our culture's values. Those who have stayed true to their vows, who have made loving and lasting marriages, are still considered, albeit often grudgingly, to have taken the better way. Just as many Gentile converts were attracted to the moral order and discipline offered by the people of the book, so too do people today look to the churches for moral inspiration and a better way.

So what kind of sexual morality are we, the Church, actually offering in these dark times? A subversive stance towards the "traditional" family which, in our society, has become an inward-looking anti-social institution? Or are we offering the optimism and the risks of the early churches' perceptions of family, community and the body? These last did not, as I hope to have suggested in this chapter, promote values and conduct acceptable to the convenience of prevailing power structures. It seems to me that if we succeed in reimposing our rules without the full-blooded challenges to "the world" in which they evolved we will have done nothing more than re-establish a Christian moral imperialism which is no more "moral" than the Crusades and witch-hunts of old.

Or are we in fact offering the *fin de siècle* cynical sexual code of the old Hellenistic dualism? This too "upheld marriage and family life" in its own dreary, utilitarian way.

Jesus was indeed pointing to a theological dimension of marriage – a vision of reconciliation between the earthly institution and the mystical union it signifies. It is given to each generation to realize it.

3

The Way of Negation

What went ye into the wilderness to see? A reed shaken
in the wind? But what went ye out for to see? A man clothed
in soft raiment? behold, they that wear soft clothing are
in kings' houses. (Matt. ll:7–8)

During the first phase of humanity men and women are
confined to the physical act of giving and the concern with
reproduction; and around that fundamental act they gradually develop a growing nimbus of spiritual exchanges.
At first it was no more than an imperceptible fringe, but
the fruitfulness and mystery of union gradually find their
way into it; and it is on that side of the nimbus that the
balance ultimately comes to rest. However, at that very
moment, the centre of physical union from which the light
emanated is seen to be incapable of further expansion. (Teil-
lard de Chardin, *Towards the Future*)

All over the world there are millions of men and women who
do not, nor ever will, make sexual, genital love. Many more
will never marry, bear or father children. Of these many, past
and present, some are Christian and have chosen their celibacy
in obedience to their faith.

I am not one of those who believe that the virgin state
is automatically a deprived one, still less that when freely
embraced, with or without religious faith, it is unnatural –
that in a healthy society, free from hang-ups, especially
religious ones, everybody, as the song says, would be happily
"doin' it". Those who do think so will long have lost interest
in this book's arguments. I do however set out to consider
the "case against" Christian sexual teaching and a powerful

argument in this case rests on the fact that, historically, this teaching has been formulated and taught almost exclusively by those who do not "do it" at all! This objection is raised not only in ignorance or hostility towards Christian tradition; faithful laypeople, too, ask,: "Why should a clerical hierarchy with no personal responsibility for marital/family relationships tell the rest of us how to conduct this area of our lives?"

When Milton wrote "It was for many ages that marriage lay in disgrace with most of the ancient doctors as a work of the flesh . . . wholly denied to priest and disswaded to all,"[1] he spoke for a Protestant Enlightenment which had been dearly bought and was still everywhere under threat. The imposition of mandatory celibacy on the Roman Catholic priesthood perpetuates a widespread suspicion that the Church really believes in its heart that celibacy is a holier and more respected calling than marriage.

The spiritual and political power that has accrued to virginity has been challenged and scrutinized in recent years as never before. Laypeople and clerics alike ask whether the Church is well-served by a "two-tier system" of holiness. The debate is taking place within a culture which no longer views sexuality as a "lower" part of the self which must be repressed in order to cultivate our higher moral and intellectual faculties. Sexuality is now seen as an integral part of our human personhood which we cannot "disown" without damaging our psychic health.

Protestantism today tends to treat the Church's long exaltation of virginity – a period which lasted nearly a millenium – as an embarrassing aberration which has nothing very helpful to say about sex. There is a tendency in Protestant marriage-teaching to skip over this period and return to the robust affirmativeness of Scripture (although this dismissiveness is somewhat inconsistent since theologians, both Catholic and Protestant, draw heavily on the Doctors of the medieval Church in all other matters).

Writings which take a broader historical approach to sexual questions see asceticism in terms of the dualisms Christianity absorbed from the Hellenistic world. It is important to see – as this chapter sets out to show – why dualism became so deeply embedded. But this line of enquiry is also somewhat biased since it ignores the sexist dualism that has throughout the centuries been closely interwoven with asceticism. Realizing that dualism is *never* class or gender neutral, feminist theologians have looked long and hard at the connection between ascetic ideologies and the oppression of women in Christian culture.

Some early feminist polemic paid scant attention to theological concepts like spiritualistic dualism and treated monasticism as nothing more than an institutionalized expression of gynaephobia. While I do not subscribe to this view it is not a perspective to be dismissed out of hand, for by drawing attention to some of the monastic fathers' diatribes against women, feminism generally has drawn attention to a misogyny which has been insufficiently acknowledged in the Church's official history and hagiographical texts. They have also shown the degree to which popular consciousness has been shaped by these negative messages (far more than "official" orthodoxy). In an institution which claims to be a true, living reflection of the divine, the medium really *is* the message; or, in biblical language, by our fruits are we known, and some proper penitence is in order for the damage and denigration that we the Church have inflicted, particularly and specifically on women over and above that inflicted on the love between women and men.

Whatever critical stance we adopt towards our Christian past, it surely goes without saying that the Church's claim that it has always, unambiguously, upheld the holy and honourable estate of matrimony is rendered patently untrue by the centuries-long elevation of virginity.

But I have also come to be surprised by the richness and

variety of the ideas asceticism carried and the forms it took during its long and complicated history. Asceticism was in ascendance during the most formative period of Christian language and theology; it absorbed the most brilliant minds and fervent spirits of Christendom for more than half of our history. Our most treasured works of art – those paintings and sculptures that draw people of all religious persuasions or none to the churches and museums of Europe – were created under its aegis. The influence of asceticism has been momentous throughout major periods of *all* religious cultures. We find, even after four centuries of sustained rejection in the West – first by Reformed and later by Enlightenment thought – that the ascetic impulse has not disappeared. So rather than allowing ourselves to be locked into stances of defending or vilifying the tradition, we need, as Rosemary Ruether suggests, "to recognise our own analogues to ascetic practices by which we today attempt to solve similar problems to those which beset our ancestors."[2]

The apostle Paul counselled chastity "in view of the present distress". It was in the struggle between the "powers and principalities" of the pagan world that the ascetic ideal first came into prominence in the Church. The first Christians fervently believed that the political world was on a catastrophe course and saw themselves as living in the "end-time" before the return of Christ. Our own society is similarly traumatized by catastrophe; we live amidst political decay and ecological disaster. The AIDS virus, which has afflicted the body of individuals is a particular and powerful analogue of our own "present distress". Total chastity is required of those who carry the virus. For the rest of us the only way we can ensure our own safety in this present trouble is by establishing faithful, monogamous unions. These were as I see it the grounds on which Paul taught the importance of chastity; both within marriage, where it stood as a sign of the integrity of the body, and by giving value to the celibacy to which some early Christians clearly felt themselves called. The first priority of all was to build up the body of Christ to prepare for his coming reign.

It is only in this context: a conviction that the health of the individual body is inextricably bound up with the health and well-being of the whole body; faith in a Saviour who *loved* the world and the flesh, loved it so much that he took on its shame and finitude and raised it to glory, that I believe the Church can dare to lay claim to its traditional teachings as a source of healing in the world today.

Many people see the requirement of chastity, either in marriage or out of it, as nothing more than a curb on pleasure and spontaneity. The Church's history has laid it open to the suspicion of its having a major investment in people "not doing it". The renewed claims of Christianity to the wisdom of its sex ethics are further unconvincing to people because they are often presented in a "moralistic" way ; loaded with individualistic notions of blame and responsibility. All too often both Church and society exhibit a dualistic impulse to project the disease away from its own body on to the body of the sinful, sensual world stewing in the juice of its own corruption, as one vociferous Christian policeman put it.

The question whether this is true, or whether in fact body-rejecting attitudes are built into the Christian ideal or a perversion of it, is of more than academic interest. It is a matter, finally, whether the Christian faith itself offers all people, married and single, AIDS sufferers and all our children, moral resources to draw on to purchase freedom, wholeness and life more abundant. But these resources have to be recovered from history: a history in which struggles for power and domination have clustered around the questions of priestly celibacy, gender roles and the place of marriage.

Asceticism did not originate in biblical faith; the word is Greek in origin meaning "exercise" and it appears only once in the New Testament, in 1 Corinthians 9:24–25, where Paul compares the Christian life to the games and urges Christians to "run the race" with the discipline and training that athletes submit themselves to.

Nor, more significantly, does it appear in the writings of any major religious culture until around the fifth century BC when the first (recorded) intimations of immortality stirred in the human soul. Mortality was till then accepted as a God-given part of the human condition. Ancient Near East and Mediterranean peoples invested their religious hopes in the renewal of life within the cycle of the seasons and the wise governance of society.

But as more and more peoples and cultures became swept into the military empires of Greece and Rome, pride and hope in their societies faded. We see the experience of political humiliation and cultural loss reflected in a widespread retreat from naturalistic, "this worldly" religious hopes towards a more sombre spiritual and intellectual reflection on the "change and decay in all around". Ascetic disciplines were first and everywhere conceived and practised as a way of transcending the sadness and corruption of the world by withdrawing from material existence to focus on a world beyond history; a world to which the individual transcendent "soul" could ascend. The disciplines of fasting, prayer and sexual abstinence were seen as ways of bearing witness to this "other" world.

However, human beings saw this ideal reality, and their relationship to it, in different ways in biblical times. After the death of Alexander the Great in 303 BC when the glory that was Greece began to fade in the loss of her proud city states, "other worldly" asceticism, a renunciation of earthly ties for "pure" contemplation, became the dominant philosophical ideal.

Judaism, which had undergone diaspora and even more humiliating defeat, continued to envisage the "future perfect" as a state to be achieved here on earth: the idea of a world *beyond* decay was anyway foreign to Hebrew thought. It was their rootedness in a this-worldly Messianic hope which informed the asceticism that developed in late Judaism and early Christianity. Celibacy was envisaged, in Ruether's words, "not simply in the sense of pleasure denial, but in the sense of resistance to worldly preoccupations, (as) one central way of symbolizing the anticipation of that age when there would be 'neither marrying nor giving in marriage'".[3] Christ's resurrection was the ultimate vindication of this hope. It was their idea that humans beings grow *through* suffering rather than by "rising above it" that set early Christian ascetics apart from schools like the Stoics who came to prominence in Imperial Rome.

One's stance towards Christian ideas is clearly informed by one's reverence, or otherwise, for Classical thought. This leads us into a cultural argument to which I cannot do justice within the scope of this book. There are, however, one or two points to keep in mind as we proceed. As already mentioned, the way terms like "Hellenistic dualism" are used to explain *away* tendencies we now wish to reject in Christianity. But it was into the Graeco–Roman world that Christianity moved and it is in fact impossible to establish exact points of interpenetration of ideas: it was an essentially *Roman* faith and order which eventually prevailed over the Jewish form. All this is further complicated by the fact that Christianity penetrated the Classical world at what was, even for its most ardent devotees, the point of its decline. After the death of Augustus (in Jesus' own time) Roman order quickly descended into tyranny.

Until Gibbon's monumental study, *The Decline and Fall of the Roman Empire*, published in the late eighteenth century, late Roman civilization was almost entirely seen through the somewhat hostile eyes of Christian history. Gibbon, however, returned his readers to a first-century world in which many people saw "these Christians" as weird and barbaric people who in their neglect of civic duty and decorum, particularly that of marriage and procreation – made the world a good deal *less* civilized. Some modern historians believe that Christianity actually contributed to the decline of civilization by rejecting Rome's own revival movements, such as Stoicism, for their masochistic obsession with death and martyrdom.

This was not, however, the world Jesus moved in. It can be safely said that the people to whom Jesus ministered had little interest in past or present glories of Rome and that the early Jesus Movement offered resources by which people could overcome the callousness and cruelty of life under the Caesars.[4] Although his lifestyle was a provocatively "marginal" one, Christ himself, "winebibber, friend of publicans and sinners" was not an ascetic of any kind. But his movement was heralded by one: the astute desert Baptist, and drew great strength from John's own Jewish (Essene) tradition. A uniquely Christian asceticism, the one Jesus urged on all his disciples, is best summed up in his call: "If any one would come after me, let him deny himself and take up his cross and follow me" (Mark 8:34), which emphasizes both the rigour of self-denial and its real purpose and prize – the athlete's prize of union with Christ.

Jesus commended celibacy only once when he referred to those who "have made themselves eunuchs for the Kingdom of heaven's sake". It is in Matthew (19:12), the Gospel "for the Jews", that this teaching occurs. Jesus' warning that "not all men receive this precept, but only those to whom it is given" (v.11) was well founded. This perplexing passage has frequently been taken as a glorification of sexual renunciation. (Origen, was one of the early fathers who received it literally and had himself castrated.)

But Jesus' statement taken as a whole and in context speaks of a new freedom and *in*clusiveness (the kind mentioned earlier, which we desperately need to recover). The first two categories of "eunuchs" Jesus referred to, those born impotent and those who were made so by men, were accursed in the old dispensation. What Christ is stressing, as Eric Fuchs explains:

> is that from now on the presence of the kingdom makes it possible to live marriage as a grace and not merely a natural state having human laws ... To confirm this declaration, Jesus alludes to three situations which are in fact not "natural"; in addition to the two categories of eunuchs disqualified by Judaism ... Jesus posits a third category, one in which the renunciation of marriage is voluntary ... Thus both celibacy and marriage, because of the Kingdom, cease being mere natural realities or destinies to be submitted to, and point to the grace which makes human freedom possible. *It is freely chosen celibacy which guarantees that marriage is itself a free choice; it is marriage lived as grace calling for faithfulness that guarantees that celibacy is not a curse ... but that it can be recognized by some as their vocation.*[5] [italics mine]

Paul, too, upheld the value and integrity of vocational celibacy as liberation from the old order (far too enthusiastically, in many people's judgement). But just as he foresaw the conflict between new family life under Christ and the patterns and obligations of family ties in the world, so too, as we saw particularly in his writings to the Corinthians, did he realize that Christian asceticism could also go the "way of the world" by buying into the comforting dualisms in which Classical thought was steeped and which underpinned all its social, intellectual and spiritual ideas, *including* its concept and practice of asceticism, which was often both escapist and élitist. As marriage could bring the faithful worldly troubles, so, Paul realized, could their sexual renunciation lead them into the temptation of seeing themselves as "set above" the worldly concerns of "ordinary" Christians. *This* world had been claimed by Christ and must be won for him and so there could be no opting out of bodily existence, for we come to know him through his body, which is in the world and is the world.

Nor could there be "disowning" of sexual bodiliness. Christ's was a bridal body of which we are *all* living parts. Paul stressed this by using explicitly sexual language to describe Christ's relationship to the Church; the bridal body taken to himself and made perfect (Ephesians 5:25–27). We are all "sexual", indeed all female in him. As long as the Christian community saw itself in this way – and by the time the New Testament was completed in the second century AD this rich, often highly sensual, imagery prevailed – there could be no "two-tier system" of holiness.

Christianity has, at its best, understood and taught a proper balance between the ascetics' Way of Negation and the Way of Affirmation. This balance rests on the very foundation of monotheistic faith and is unique to it. It is indicated in 1 John 4:12 "No man hath seen God at any time. If we love one another God dwelleth in us, and his love is perfected in us." The ascetics' Way of Negation witnesses to the first part of this sentence: Judaism's primary awareness of God's not-knownness. Human experience only provides partial, incomplete images of God who dwells beyond as well as within our understanding and our relationships with one another. This not-knownness can be honoured by non-attachment to the things of the world through the voluntary poverty and chastity to which all Christians are, in different ways, called.

The church seemed to hold on to a holistic view of asceticism in its first two centuries. Sanctity was not then synonymous with sexual renunciation and early Christian literature celebrated women and men as prophets and martyrs, teachers and leaders. Married and single, all were able to sit lightly, as Paul had been at such pains to encourage them to do, to the world and its civic/family obligations. Even unto death.

It is significant that a very particular heroism was accorded those women martyrs who spurned marital ties when these conflicted with membership of their new chosen family in Christ. An early popular heroine was Thecla, a young woman from Iconium whose story is told in a second-century apocryphal writing.[6] Converted by Paul, who commissioned her to "go and teach the word of God", Thecla resisted the combined pressure of family and state authority by breaking her marriage contract to take off on her colourful adventures. Perpetua left husband and newborn son to be martyred (in 202) with her slave-sister Felicitas whose own child was born in the condemned cell. (Their canonization also shows that it was still possible, then, to be female, married and a mother as well as a leader in the Christian community.)

But a two-tier system did creep in and was soon established with a vengeance. So much so that by the fourth century St Jerome could declare that virginity filled heaven and marriage the earth. He could only "praise marriage and wedlock because they beget celibates: I gather roses from thorns, gold from the earth, pearls from shells".[7] Such a metaphor clearly spells out disastrous implications for marriage, for what value is a shell from which the pearl is taken; or a celibacy so exalted above it? Paul's fears of spiritual pride were well-founded.

How and why did the once creative tension collapse into bitter opposition? A common view was that this was inevitable, that it was indeed built into the system from the start by Paul with his clear preference for celibacy. Even the most cursory reading of St Paul (and even granting the ambiguities in his writing) refuses to yield such a simplistic view. So why has it clung? Angela West offers a helpful explanation in her 1982 study of Corinthians:

> In this letter you can see Paul fighting with his back against the wall to preserve what he understood as Christian freedom. *It's important to realise that historically speaking, he*

lost [italics mine]. It was the heirs of the superspirituals ... who won. And it is very revealing to see how they have coped with Paul.[8]

As West demonstrates, one misappropriated line of Paul's – "It is better for a man not to touch a woman" – has been "the headwater in Christianity for repressive views on sex that have flowed through all branches of the church. In Western history all those who have glorified sexual austerity have pinned their doctrines on this verse".[9]

It is indeed interesting to see the many ways "Paul lost". In order to do so we must take account of the historical changes that divided Paul from the patristic superspirituals. We have to reckon not just with the "events" of history but with the problem of time itself. This, as Charles Williams says, is "*the* great problem for philosophers," "Nor", he added, "is it otherwise with the believers":

> Christianity is, always, the redemption of a point, of one particular point (of discovery). "*Now* is the accepted time; *now* is the day of salvation." In this sense there is nothing but *now*; there is no duration. We have nothing to do with duration, and yet (being mortal) we have to do with nothing but duration; between those contrasts also all the history and doctrine of Christendom lies ... The Epistles of St Paul carry that Now to the highest point of exploration and of expression. But already in the Epistles themselves something else has come in. Time existed, and time itself had, as it were, to be converted, to be rededicated towards the thing out of time.[10]

Like slavery, marriage, along with time and sin, continued to exist and its re-dedication to "the thing out of time" proved even more problematical. Pauline arguments for some sort of *modus vivendi* with the old order led, among other things, to the rededication of marriage to the patriarchal world. These are the arguments which have exercised most powerful and long-term influence on Christian marital theory. (Liberal Christians have only recently challenged Pauline fundamentalism by pointing out that if we are required to take "Wives obey your husbands" literally then we must also uphold slavery since this injunction was accompanied by one to slaves to obey their masters.)

The early missionaries' very success in preaching the Gospel to all nations meant that the Church was drawn away from its Jewish roots into the mainstream Classical world. As the Church took on the task of producing a written orthodoxy and, later, workable systems of authority, the social – and intellectual – patterns of this world became harder and harder to resist and soon gained validity in both practical and doctrinal matters.

By AD200 Christianity was still dominated by the kind of married household we see in the Church cell communities of Acts. Pliny the Younger (one of those who undertook the task of surveillance of Christian "saints" on behalf of the Empire) was clearly impressed by their moral discipline as well as their intense devotions:

(they met) regularly before dawn on a fixed day to chant verses alternately among themselves in honour of Christ as if to a god, and also to bind themselves by oath, not for any criminal purpose, but to abstain from theft, robbery and adultery, to commit no breach of trust and not to deny a deposit when called upon to restore it.[11]

However the diverse, practical patterns of ministry they evolved – for worship, prayer, and mutual sustenance – were superseded on the one hand by larger scale, more hierarchical forms of administration, and on the other by the ascetic communities that grew up away from centres of population.

The separation of married and celibate vocations was at

first a temporary, pragmatic one. The first desert hermits fled there in order to keep the faith alive in times when it was hardest pressed. They did not see themselves as heroes, since they had chosen the desert over the martyr" crown. Nor did they practise their ascetic disciplines in splendid isolation: the first followers of the Baptist shared the richness of their intense mystical experience with the whole community. They took over the practical works of mercy by collecting and distributing alms. There was a lot more coming and going between the desert and the city than is commonly realized and those people who sought spiritual counsel from the desert fathers included married Christians who did not seek to join the desert way of life on a permanent basis.

Furthermore, as Peter Brown points out, the most rigorous early ascetics – John Chrystostom and Clement of Alexandria, for example, – warmly defended the place of marriage in Christian life.

By accepting marriage, and, with marriage the enduring structures of the Christian household, Clement was well aware that he was also advocating a peculiar and necessary brand of Christian courage, for the married could not die as the ascetic could, unshaken by the most terrible wrench of all, fear for the fate of one's wife/husband and children.

Clement went further than praise for the married, he actually sought to merge the City world of Acts with the desert by establishing structures of familial monasticism.[12] This is a very different picture from the one we have inherited from (later) hagiography focusing on the fathers' triumphs over the lascivious "world" they had "left behind". Sexual desires were understandably a torment for some, as has been vividly recorded in the Saints' lives, but there were far more immediate demons – hunger, persecution and social injustice – for them to wrestle with.

However, as time passed and Christianity became "respectable", the desert holy ones, and the egalitarian counter-culture they embodied, were institutionalized into monasticism. The monastic communities were ordered by the "rules" and answerable to the hierarchy rather than the people and so became more and more enclosed and further separated from the world of marriage and families. The ideal Christian life, of shared bread, work and prayer was no longer available to all Christians but only to this celibate élite. There was a place for marriage in the kingdom but it became inevitably a "second best" as spiritual authority and later, when the monasteries became centres of learning, doctrinal authority too came to reside not in the whole community but in cloistered chastity. Lifelong virginity became required of the Church's holy ones: primacy of honour and special powers of intercession were only granted to those who had chosen this path.

Paul can certainly be said to have "lost" in this regard, for he had vigorously repudiated notions of a celibate élite. Élitism, of course, pervades all human groups and creeps into most religious cultures. But the validity it gained in Christianity, whose teachings about mutual service so explicitly undermined it, calls for particular repentance and amendment. Overcoming élitism is of the utmost importance today, for along with other Christians I am not "against" celibacy *per se*, only its claim to be "better than" marriage; a claim that has fundamentally distorted the Christian concept of ministry as well as the Christian sex ethic. (None of this is meant to deny either the humility or the astonishingly sacrificial living of individuals who have ministered within monasticism.)

The idea of virginity as a higher state was first preached by the gnostics. These "heirs of the superspirituals" gained more and more ground in the post-Pauline Church. They gathered themselves into sects under various gnostic teachers and a major controversy arose between the early fathers and the gnostic schools which came to dominate theological and ethical discourse during the first four centuries AD.

As we saw in chapter 2 gnostic/superspiritual ideas thrived on the comforting conviction that the body itself did not really, finally matter, a conviction as often expressed in rigid asceticism as in "anything goes" permissiveness. Many of the fathers' pronouncements about the place of marriage (including the warm defence issued by Clement of Alexandria referred to above) were formulated specifically in order to combat the gnostic heresy that acclaimed "the transcendence of sexual desire as nothing less than a resurrection of the self". The libertine tendency of superspiritualism resurfaced in second-century Christianity in a form called antinomianism, a teaching which proclaimed that enlightened man is above common laws and can never "sin" no matter what he does. Many of the fathers' defences seem lukewarm, even grudging, to modern ears, but it is important to realize that they were, in fact, a positive reaction to an even greater ambivalence.

Gnosticism seriously undermined monotheism itself. As Christianity gained ground over Imperial paganism and particularly after Constantine made it the official religion of the Empire, gnostics tried to accommodate this central biblical precept to the prevailing dualisms by teaching a dual Creation/creator. They taught a belief that the world was created in error by an evil Demiurge. This idea of a dual Creation, one good and spiritual, the other trapped in fleshliness and matter, translates all too easily into convenient hierarchies where the negative elements of creation are projected on to "other" groups; women, slaves, even nature itself can all be safely despised and exploited because they only serve the sad necessities of material life. (A highly sophisticated way of having God, the "right" God, of course, on our side.)

Christian orthodoxy officially prevailed over the gnostic heresy but the wounds of so bitter and distracting a struggle so early in the Church's life remained; as did the seeds of suspicion towards sexual activity, which, once sown, sprang up again and again throughout our history. The place of marriage in the Christian life was upheld but its defence came to lie more and more in its procreative "natural law" aspects rather than in the pre-eminence of love and relationality which Christ (and Paul in his way) had taught.

The extent and nature of the gnostic legacy comes into sharpest focus when we look, as feminists scholars have done, at the anthropology of male and female which came to inform patristic sexual teaching. As dualism gained ascendancy the gnostic ideal of "life in the flesh transcended" coexisted, albeit conflictually, with the Christian vision of a "life in the flesh *transformed*". Paul's doctrine of a spiritual body was reinterpreted as a "non-bodily sort of body". Once this idea takes hold we find that it is the male body – always more easily identified with mind and spirit – which more easily fitted the ideal. The female body as source of physical being was once again securely identified with "nature". "And nature is what we are put in this world to rise above." Teilhard de Chardin put the same sentiment in more scholarly, critical and gender specific terms in his critique of the celibate system: "Logically the saint will attain the maximum of self-perfection by a minimum use of matter – and most particularly of matter in its most virulent form – the feminine."[13]

St Ambrose (fourth century), one of the four great Doctors of the Latin church, clearly accepted this equation: "She who does not believe is a woman and should be designated with the name of her sex, whereas she who believes progresses to perfect manhood, to the measure of the adulthood of Christ."[14] This image owes its origin to Plato's *Symposium*, which conceives of a ladder whereby the soul ascends from human love to the divine. Whoever speaks it, this hierarchical language spells spiritual and social disaster for all women, "sexual" or virgin. The latter were, in ways that were never imposed on men, required to transcend rather than discipline their sexuality. A motif of "de-sexed" female spiritual progression appears throughout hagiography from Perpetua's dream, where she becomes a male athlete in order to defeat the devil; to the warrior Joan and subsequent virgin martyrs who all saw themselves as needing disciplines over and above the practice of chastity if they were to progress "to perfect manhood".[15]

St Jerome in the early fifth century pointed the way in the advice and counsel he offered to the coterie of aristocratic Roman ladies he trained in the ascetic life. He urged them to practise the most rigorous mortifications, elaborating on matters of dress, diet and deportment with pedagogic thoroughness. Modern commentators have noted that Jerome's fasting programme would have induced amenorrhoea (cessation of the menstrual cycle) in an average woman. It is clear that the programme was designed to blot out any vestige of female sexual allure. In Jerome the best and the worst of Christian asceticism are uniquely combined and personified. Jerome lived through the final periods of the churches' persecution and into its Constantinian establishment under which he exercised his great scholastic gifts: Jerome's Vulgate, his translation of the Bible into Latin, is an unsurpassed achievement of the early Church. Some of his early life was spent in the desert and while the desert bred the fanaticism which undoubtedly informed his teachings and his counsels – Jerome was much given to expounding his hallucinatory experiences of being beset by lustful wantons – it also bred a heroic gentleness and courage. Jerome, commonly portrayed with his lion, reminds us of the magic kindness that existed between the fathers and the wild beasts.

It certainly took courage to defy Roman marriage customs. We can easily forget that self-chosen, consecrated virginity for *women* was a totally new religious idea which had to be defended in the pagan world. The pressure on women to bear children was intense in the ancient world, particularly in the late Roman Empire where five children per woman was the number required to keep the population at an acceptable level. Jerome must have been a real thorn in the flesh to late Roman society since his high-born ladies would have been highly valuable breeding stock. Think of the grief and outrage of middle-class parents today when their children are removed from the sphere of their families' influence by cults like the Moonies.

Roman robustness and rigour in matters of marriage eroded as the Empire crumbled into decay. The Roman divorce laws, respected to this day for their humane tolerance, were increasingly abused and trivialized by this time; Jerome apparently knew of one Roman matron who married her twenty-third husband, becoming his twenty-first wife. Jerome and his ilk offered them a way out of all that corruption. Perhaps it is because his involvement was intensely pastoral and personal that Jerome's teaching – and the images of women conveyed by it – has remained so vivid and memorable. Jerome seemed to lack the fear of women, the desire to keep them at arm's length that we associate with later monastic purity. He treated his women trainees as colleagues and equals in study and prayer; that is once their feet were set firmly on the path to virginity. In this sense and in the sense that he saw virginity as liberation from bondage Jerome was a true heir of Paul. He fulminated against the distracting, repetitive and demeaning nature of housework in a way that would gladden the heart of many a modern Martha! But "chastity", the word, and the grace, was no longer applicable to the virtuously, faithfully wedded. Jerome reserves all the warmth and enthusiasm traditionally accorded to the biblical "virtuous woman" for the virgins and widows under his tutelage.

And there was no middle path. The opposite of a good chaste woman was the strumpet. In this Jerome followed Tertullian (late second century) the first influential teacher to mistake Paul's notorious opening of 1 Corinthians 7 by lump-ing all sexually active women together in harlotry. Tertullian, although reputedly far more moderate than Jerome in his championship of celibacy, was one of the first to introduce the idea of Eve as "first fallen". He denounced women as the Devil's gateway, urging them to remember that they were the "destroyers of God's image man". It really had to be better for men not to touch them at all. This is how Tertullian reconciles his decidedly unbiblical perspective with the teaching of the Church on marriage:

It is laws which seem to make the difference between marriage and fornication through the diversity of illicitness [a fair comment perhaps in the light of the state of marriage. However he continues] not through the nature of the thing itself. Besides what is the thing which takes place in all men and women to produce marriage and fornication? Commixture of the flesh of course; the concupiscence whereof the Lord put on the same footing with fornication.... Accordingly, the best thing for a man is not to touch a woman and accordingly the virgin is the principal sanctity, because it is free from affinity with fornication.[16]

So if faithful, monogamous marriage cannot save us from moral depravity what possible good is it? Providing the best environment for children to be raised in? Procreation, marriage's chief line of defence, was obviously a good excuse but not a very convincing one in the earliest days of the Church when the "appointed time" for the world's end was believed to be close. Later when the Church saw its central task as upholding the purity of Christian life in a licentious pagan environment it was still more concerned with quality rather than quantity of life. Hence the idea, put forth by Jerome and his contemporaries, that a woman's loss of sexual purity

87

could be compensated by producing virgin offspring gained force.

The Church was to be forced out of this uncompromising corner by a new powerful school of Gnosticism which surfaced in the third century. The Manichaeans scorned sex precisely because it *did* lead to childbirth and urged Christians who could not manage total abstinence at least to refrain from procreation. This went to the heart of the matter of the goodness of Creation itself. The Genesis command to "increase and multiply" had to be defended against the extreme pessimism – and the potential permissiveness of this sect. The task of combating Manichaeism fell largely to Augustine whose sexual teaching set the stage of Christian thought for centuries to come. Augustine upheld the theological value of marriage against this Manichaean attack by unilaterally upholding its procreative function. Augustine was a bishop and his towering influence marks the beginning of the long era in which Christian writings come almost exclusively from men at the top of the church's hierarchy; an era in which those at the top who do not "do it" started telling the rest of us how to: which was as little as possible! – only for children to people heaven!

The Prayer Book's threefold purpose of marriage – procreation, remedy for sin and symbol of unity – was first formulated by Augustine . But the symbol of unity purpose of marriage whose primacy was upheld both by Paul and Christ himself, remain undeveloped in Augustinian teaching. From now on everything conspired to exclude sexual *love* in the discussion of Christian ethics and one of the most significant developments of Indo-European culture, the juxtaposition of love and marriage, was set in reverse. We are firmly in the world of pagan stoicism where pleasure is the enemy and "too much love for one's spouse is adultery". Add to this the unique brands of misogyny developed by the early fathers, the de-sexing of "holy" women and a derision of the carnal kind, and we have a very weird view of wives: "A good Christian is found in one and the same woman to love the creature of God whom he desires to be transformed and renewed, but to hate her in the corruptible and mortal conjugal connection, sexual intercourse and all that pertains to her as a wife."[17] Augustine goes on to compare the relations of the Christian husband to his wife with the mandate to "love our enemies"!

Much has been made of the fact that Augustine was deeply troubled by his own sexual desires. It is said that he repented his fifteen-year-long liaison with his (unnamed) mistress, and mother of his son Deodatus far more fervently than any of his youthful debaucheries. He was appalled by the anatomical facts of lust, believing that the seat of "disordered affection due to sin" is the penis, which by having what might be called a life of its own was for him "the literal embodiment of that 'law of the members that wars against the law of the minds'"[18] Augustine's graphically-described horror is treated with embarrassment by most patristic historians. For women, however, unembarrassed by this troublesome organ, Augustine provides the most graphic evidence for the feminist observation that our culture's definitions of sex are male-derived.

But can we dismiss Augustine's hang-up as a personal foible? Or was it a culture-bound one, that is "he had trouble relating to women like all men of his time"? It was perfectly consistent with the entire system of theological anthropology which he inherited and created.

The beleaguerment of the Church itself must surely have contributed, as much as their personal foibles, to the fathers' pessimism about sex. The old problems of time and place weighed particularly heavily upon Augustine. With the era of martyrdom now long in the past the Christian struggle for perfection was no longer intelligible as a brave struggle against a corrupt, licentious environment. The Enemy was now unmistakably Within: in the bodies of individuals like himself beset by sexual shame and in the body of the Church itself torn apart by heresy and internal strife. Augustine's North African see was at the eye of most of fifth century's schismatic storms.[19]

The old enemy without – the pagan world had taken on new menacing dimensions. Augustine presided over a Church poised at the edge of what we call the Dark Ages. His great *City of God* was written when the barbarians were at the very gates of Rome. For Augustine, educated in the schools of Italy, Rome was not the corrupt pagan power it had been for Paul and the early fathers, but the cradle of his Christianity and of "civilization as he knew it". Rome's decline and fall were now his own and the Church's sorrow and shame, for it was in and through Rome that the Church, like Adam in Eden, had been given dominion over the world. Thus it was that by Augustine's time, as Charles Williams writes, "Adam ... suddenly returned" to Christianity. Sin continued and there was no cheap escape from it. Augustine concluded that to refuse the ancient heritage of guilt for the Fall is to cut ourselves off from mankind as certainly as to refuse the new principle of forgiveness. "It was now seen as necessary to submit to the one as freely as the other."[20]

Augustine approached his biblical ancestry on its own terms of moral tragedy, guilt and judgement. But he proposed submissions to the old patriarchal order that would have been scandalous to Paul. The right of a married woman to "abjure the marriage bed", which Jerome and earlier fathers had upheld so enthusiastically, was denied by Augustine under whose teaching male headship became an absolute and central dogma. And her desire, if it shall be for God and not all for a husband – too bad since he rules anyway. Augustine's ascetical obsession with rational, passion-free, procreation–only intercourse, combined with his patriarchal rejection of female autonomy, even led him to rationalize patriarchal polygamy on the grounds that the biblical worthies felt no lust but were only obeying God's command to "increase and multiply"! The New Testament's sexual radicalism and Paul's own proclamation of moral liberty were the casualties of this renewed accommodation with patriarchal privilege.[21]

Here we have it: the old Adam's sexist double standard completely restored within the new superspiritual asceticism which saw in virginity the only sure route to heaven. Emptied of spiritual meaning monogamy was now seen purely in terms of damage limitation, the only thinkable, but always inadequate compromise with the flesh.

Augustine's view remained the norm throughout the early Middle Ages, which yielded little further theological reflection on sex and marriage. Extant writings from this period consist mainly of advice to priests on how best to implement Augustinian precepts through the confessional.

The "icy overtones" of Augustinianism were somewhat thawed by the twelfth century. The Fourth Lateran Council (1215) declared that: "Not only virgins and celibates, but also married people who please God by right faith and good conduct merit to arrive at eternal happiness". In the teachings of Thomas Aquinas, the Church's chief spokesman on these matters in the thirteenth century, "good conduct" was still defined as intercourse practised only for procreation, but in Thomism the taint of fallenness was largely removed from conjugal intercourse. Reason, not shame, was now the watchword governing sexual ethics.

The High Middle Ages (which ran from the eleventh to the fifteenth centuries) saw a dramatic enlightenment in Western thought as a whole which made possible a wider, more systematic and positive theological reflection on marriage. C. S. Lewis describes this age as one of revolutionary change compared with which the sixteenth century Renaissance was but "a mere ripple on the surface of literature".[22] The intellectual and spiritual vitality it engendered were sustained from a number of sources which, in their different ways, contributed to a changed sexual consciousness. The works of old Classical masters were recovered by European scholars. Aristotelean metaphysics and natural science were quickly assimilated by figures like Abelard and Aquinas and other leading exponents of a new systematic theology.

The christening of Europe after the Dark Ages provides the backdrop to this history: the faith permeated all aspects of medieval life and the fathers acquired a new dominion over the world. Though Christianity cannot remotely be said to behave more Christianly when its back is no longer against the wall, it can more comfortably and creatively absorb secular ideas, which are in turn more easily spread in times of relative stability. From now on the development of Christian attitudes to sex can only be adequately understood in the light of the Church's skill in co-opting new strains of secular thought. These too arose from a rediscovery of the Classics. Latin poetry, notably that of Ovid, from the happier times of the early Roman Empire enjoyed a revival. Inspired by Ovid's light-hearted discourses the first seeds of a Western Art of Love were sown in Southern France in the early twelfth century. The courtly poets celebrated the ennobling power of sexual passion. Body and soul, as they saw it, need no longer be locked in mortal combat for the ability to love nobly and passionately is that which sets us apart from the "brute beasts of creation".

Just as a new language of the heart found a new poetic metre so too did the whole world of letters move forward into more flexible, sophisticated forms. It was the Renaissance of Classical sciences that had the deepest influence on the didactic high theology of Aquinas. He enthusiastically adopted the naturalism and empiricism of Aristotelean thought which ought to have undermined the androcentricism of the fathers. Thomas, however, built his theology of gender from Aristotle's biology (which was far less advanced than that of his contemporaries). Aristotle believed that the complete human being was contained in the male sperm, owing nothing to the mother but her function as nesting-box. This gave a "scientific" imprimatur to notions of women's incompleteness and passivity. Thomas followed Aristotle in asserting that a girl child resulted as an accident to the male sperm which ought to contain a "complete", that is, male human being, in the image of its Creator. Though women's necessity cannot be denied – being the only nesting-boxes around – Thomas believed that for all other activities, intellectual, work, men would be better served by a male helpmeet. It is anybody's guess whether Thomas, an oblate at five years old who seems to have had no hostility to women or to sex and was in every way sympathetic to the new enquiring spirit of the age, would have arrived at this negative theology of gender if he had had the proper information.

A denial of women's positive role in generation was extended to post-natal life. Thomas recommended that a child should be given to his father after weaning that is at the age of three or thereabouts for education and training in the Christian life. Thus modern arguments for monogamous union, which rest heavily upon the need for stable upbringing by both parents, were completely absent in Thomism and do not appear for another three hundred years or so.

Twelfth century love lyricism was absorbed into prevailing concepts of Christian piety with an astonishing ease and eloquence. The courtly poets did not attempt a rejuxtaposition of love and marriage; it was axiomatic that the purity of passion they exalted was adulterous. Nor did the Church at this period demand it: the nature of feudal marriage, itself procreation-centred, precluded any serious dialogue between the two. The poets' lyrical intensity was instead transmuted into devotion to Mary and the rich Christian mysticism she inspired in the early twelfth century.

A digression: readers will have noticed that Mary has not so far been mentioned. This is not because I wish to deny her central role in shaping the Church's attitude to sexuality and gender, just the opposite. The fact is that in so far as Mary has served the cause of monogamy at all, she has done so only comparatively recently and *always* somewhat obliquely, as we shall see. Theology, belief and ethical teaching (as opposed to popular piety) rarely focused on Mary in early Christianity. Neither Jesus nor Paul is recorded as having suggested a special "role" for Mary in the Church, indeed neither ever mentioned her by name. For the early Christian ascetics she did provide a model of chastity but it was not the only or even the dominant one. She only came fully into the picture and to her title of Our Lady, Mother of God, in the period we are now assessing. Monogamy has never been seen as a particular Marian virtue; in fact she has done more to obscure its significance than to promote it. Because of this, and because Mariology is too vast and complex to do justice to in this book, I would like, at this point, simply to pay tribute to Marina Warner's *Alone of All Her Sex*.[23] By showing us how the different aspects of Mary's cult rose to meet the exigencies of history and to shore up the power of the Church, Warner's research has added immeasurably to my own understanding of Christian history and my own grasp of the subject of this book. Her outstanding scholarship has been an irreplaceable resource for all women who shared, unarticulated but deep in our souls, Warner's "new intimation that in the very celebration of the perfect human woman, both humanity and women were subtly denigrated".[24] This paradox was never more painfully apparent than in the twelfth century when Mary's cult rose to its zenith in her personification of the Church as Bride.

In Bernard of Clairvaux's ecstatic exposition of the Song of Songs, Mary gathers into herself all the nuptial imagery of Old and New Testaments. In a sermon cycle preached over eighteen years to the monks of Clairvaux, Bernard creates a mystical system of breathtaking power and beauty in which the Christian is transfigured by a love which, like that of the

Song, is stronger than death: "I love because I love, I love that I may love. A great thing is love, provided only that it return to its principle, look to its origin, and flowing backwards towards its source draw then the pure waters wherewith it may flow unendingly". There could be no more lovely defence of a faithful Christian union than this. But for Bernard the only "pure", disinterested love was the monk's chastity. Only by this, he says, can the soul leap towards God. Carnal desire – which the canticle itself evokes so numinously – disfigures the soul and blocks the path to primal harmony. But both loves are expressed in the same language; images of merging, fusing, dissolving in desire flow through Bernard's devotions. For the first time, then, we see one strand of biblical tradition, the Way of Affirmation, totally appropriated by the other Way of Negation. We talk of the Devil having all the best tunes but it is a bit much when a saint speaking with the tongue of angels does it! Warner's more scholarly judgment is harsh:

> The most immediate act of fusion, the one experience every human being has of combining two in one, is forbidden. The icon of Mary and Christ side by side is one of the Christian church's most polished deceptions: it is the very image and hope of earthly consummated love used to give that kind of love the lie. Its undeniable power and beauty do not heal: rather the human sore is chafed and exposed.[25]

The darker side of Bernard's fanatical devotion can be seen in the hatred he bore for heretics. Catharism was one new movement which could not be co-opted by Bernard's Church or by the forces of the feudal state but had to be eradicated. It is worth considering here because, unlike the nascent secular Romance on the one side and the challenge of classical Reason on the other, it actually succeeded in challenging Christian sexual orthodoxy. Furthermore the outcome of the Church's

95

long crusade against the Cathar heresy had profound and long-term effects on European political history as well as its sexual and social mores.

Cathar communities flourished throughout southern France in the eleventh century and found many adherents among the higher ranks of society. It was a gnostic movement, essentially a revival of Manichaeism and manifested the same rigorous dualism which had informed earlier forms of gnostic asceticism: an absolute disdain for sexuality which leads to a "permissive" morality in practice. For the Cathars, marriage and procreation signified submission to the world and the flesh and so were a more serious offence against their ideal of non-attachment than "natural" sexual pleasure.

There was on the face of it nothing very new in all this. But the old battle lines of Christianity's war against the gnostics had shifted dramatically by the time of the Cathars. Their hostility towards marriage was not now noticeably more virulent than the Christian Church's own. Furthermore while absolute chastity and rigid ascetic disciplines were required of the "top" Cathars – the *parfaites* – their "two-tier system" was distinctly less oppressive towards the "simple faithful" than the prurient disciplinarianism of an ascetic Church hierarchy.

Catharism undermined the Church's authority in ways that were highly persuasive not just to libertines and sinners but to influential people of deep spiritual and ascetic seriousness. By placing the highest value on *gnosis*, knowledge illuminated by Wisdom, Gnosticism affirms all sources of truth – intellectual, intuitive, existential – and so resists the impulse to enclose their spirituality in creeds and dogma or to invest religious, doctrinal authority in a clerical caste. Since the Wisdom they cherished was traditionally female, Sophia, women were held in the highest esteem and played an important part in all areas of Cathar community life. It would seem from the documented evidence that the Cathars created really "alternative" communities, which allowed people to live gentle, Spirit-filled lives. By upholding the humanists' more exalted view of sexuality of womanhood and by rejecting sexual shame the Cathars gave social substance to powerful new intimations of the human heart which the Church seemingly wished to crush.

It is interesting to note that the Lateran declaration (quoted above) was a declaration against Catharism. The cynical might be justified in concluding that the Church only "remembers" the sanctity of marriage when heretics call their bluff! However, the Catharic heresy was never quite obliterated. The Dominican order was founded to fight its remnants and to revive monastic fervour in the South. The Church hierarchy meanwhile turned its attention towards establishing its jurisdiction over legal aspects of marriage which led, ultimately, to a new emphasis on the sacramental character of the institution. But, with the Dominicans, the Age of Inquisition had begun and the celibate élite's power over the souls of laypeople was translated to an absolute power of life and death over their physical bodies. The stake and the torture chamber cast their shadows over all unorthodox movements for another four hundred years.

But the "new thing", the simple idea that sexual love is a source of happiness and meaning, could not be for ever contained. The celibate clerisy lost its absolute power over Christendom at the Reformation when the Church, both Protestant and Catholic, found an accommodation to a "secular" language of the heart and expanded the meaning of chastity to include the love of faithfully wedded spouses. This is the subject of chapter 4.

The question remains: how do we, a generation still in flight from the "chill shades" of ascetic teaching, "relate to" it now. I can only echo Peter Brown who ends his monumental study by asking us to:

give back to these ideas a little of the human weight they carried in their own time. When such an offering is made, the chill shades may speak to us again, and perhaps more gently than we thought they might, in the strange tongue of a long-lost Christianity. Whether they will say anything of help or comfort for our own times the readers of this book must decide for themselves.[26]

This writer has not spoken gently: my purpose is not to convey the many spiritual riches of the monastic tradition but to assess its cost to the natural human affections of women and men. But I do believe that all history carries "strange tongues" and "long-lost ideas" and that it is our job to hear them and connect them to the present. The following connections are only tenuous as yet, but I offer them here.

Over the past twenty years or so feminists and others have found not only "comfort" but inspiration in those traditions which have been submerged in the mainstream; we find these have been ones to which women have made a significant intellectual and spiritual contribution and in which they enjoyed power and privileges which were unacceptable to prevailing notions of "women's place". It was inevitable that many of these traditions (the Cathari for example) operated as heretical movements outside the Church. As Brown and others have so eloquently demonstrated, "mainstream" Christian asceticism itself began – and continued for longer than is generally imagined – as a "resistance movement"; one which was embraced with marked enthusiasm by women as an escape from the heavy burden of femaleness in ancient society. But, as we have seen, Christian asceticism gradually lost that radical direction by capitulating to the very structures it set out to resist, claiming a privileged role within the Church and the world on the grounds that their chastity was the "better" and holier way. The once creative balance between the Way of Negation and the Way of Affirmation of bodiliness could not be held: with it was lost a correct, incarnational understanding of sexual ethics and a correct understanding of celibacy as vocation.

But history also teaches us that dualistic systems seldom operate in the interests of women. So rather than simply focus, as religious histories often do, on the "special" honour and recognition women achieved as nuns (which, like Mariology itself, did not do much for the rest of us), we should give more weight than we usually do to the implications of medieval misogyny for all women, religious as well as lay. We can assume that women's experience of virginity must have been "different" to that of men. The Church actually required this to be so, as can be seen in the more disciplined and separate practice of celibacy that were imposed upon women, on the very grounds of their "otherness", their closer (and convenient) identification with "nature".

Female asceticism never became linked to power in the same way that men's did. This applies on the simple level of sexual biology; we speak of male continence, a "holding in" of sexual potency, while female virginity is associated with emptiness, barrenness. If "Man wants ... to fill: woman to be filled", men and women made different sacrifices in renouncing their sexuality. Male celibacy became linked to a priestly power and authority which was absolutely denied to women. No women's religious community could be autonomous and self-sufficient, for its sacramental life depended on the "outside intervention" of a male priest. The idea, implicit in much male monasticism, of being set above others was never so strongly emphasized to women, on whom proper humility was more often urged.

May we then conclude that monastic women had less "interest" in upholding the prevailing dualisms? Feminist research has unearthed a few rebellious spirits who succeeded in hanging on to a more holistic incarnational vision of holiness. The twelfth century Abbess Hildegarde of Bingen was a brilliant scientist, biblical scholar and spiritual teacher whose devotions were every bit as rich and joyous as Bernard's, but, as Marina Warner points out, her life's work "constitutes a rejoinder to Bernard's mystical system". Hildegarde bypassed the usual intercessory paths and identified herself with "the symbol of transcendence itself".[27] Her most memorable and original images for the visionary's relation to God came not from Scripture but from art, folk lore and nature study: she saw herself as a harp that sang as the breath of God moved through it; as a "simple feather" on the breath of God. Hildegarde shows herself to have been deeply aware of the Church's denigration of womanhood and so chose, in the teeth of the close surveillance imposed on her work, to celebrate it: she founded a community of women who in their very dress signalled their identity with the holy and the divine. Warner suggests that Hildegarde was not a maverick isolated genius:

> It is perhaps surprising that the cult of Mary is less marked in the texts of women writers of the Middle Ages, that the biblical passages which sustained her praises in the 12th and 13th Centuries were not always applied to her by nuns with the same effusions as they excited in monks. The asymmetry springs from the erotic character of the imagery: votaries' relationship to Sophia, to Holy Wisdom, was changed by the question of sex.[28]

Our own twentieth century has bred some radical, visionary nuns who have chosen, in explicitly political ways, to identify, not with the interests of the Church hierarchy but with the plight of women in our society. These women subvert the unholy alliance between those patriarchal and ascetic ideologies that have simultaneously oppressed women and robbed fleshly love of dignity and meaning. Hildegarde wrote and said nothing about marriage in the flesh; her own calling and the times she lived in precluded any great interest in the matter. But she did speaking of sexual/spiritual energy, of the beauty, integrity and meaning of bodily existence and through her speaking Hildegarde shows us the roots of a more affirmative, egalitarian sexual theology running back deep in time.

The twelfth century story that has burned most brightly down the ages *is* a "real" love story – a story of fierce and passionate fidelity and endurance. Abelard and Héloïse have been immortalized in drama, fiction and even a 1930s pop song. Their love was born not in the cloister – though it ended there – but in the heady new world of learning. Abelard taught reason as the habitation of God with humankind and dazzled the Schools of France with his brilliant mastery of logic. She, convent-bred and educated, was his pupil and equal. "You think it is the dove and the hawk, I tell you, you have seen the mating of eagles."[29] When these two came together they kindled a torch that lit all France, all Europe and scandalised the Church. Abelard pressed for marriage – she resisted, preferring "by far the name of mistress". For Héloïse, as far many of her kindred spirits today, earthly love too is only pure and disinterested when freed from contractual ties.

It ended, as it was bound to, in grief and calamity. The letters, written during their long separation, are heartrending. Each clung fiercely to their own truth – Abelard to his denial: "My love was but concupiscence and did not deserve the name", he tells her. He learned to tear his love out of his heart, as it had been torn from his body (by his castration at the hand of Héloïse's vengeful uncle). The Church, ignobly abetted by St Bernard was not satisfied at denying Abelard his priesthood; they tried to break his pride. They failed – he found a new faith and a new vocation in an obscure retreat deep in the French countryside. Here young idealists in the faith came to seek him out as they had sought out the Baptist and the early Desert fathers.

For Héloïse there was no renewed vocation : she clung to

her first and last truth – of the oneness and gift of the union with Abelard. She refused to sublimate or spiritualize a love that belonged to and with the body. The loss and mutilation rings out across the walls the Church put between them, into the world that immortalized them – as lovers – in the end.

4

Romance

How should a gospel bring glad tidings
Save by announcing what was from the
Beginning native to the heart.
Alan Ecclestone, Christmas Poem 1984.

*   *   *

Whom the gods would destroy they first make ̄ sentimental.
(Helen Waddell *Peter Abelard*)

We do not find romantic love as a basis for marriage in Scripture or the early teachings of the Church. When it first arose
as a central theme of European literature it boldly set its face
against the entire social and spiritual order. The plight of
the courtly Lover and his Lady, trapped in the rigid categories
of feudal society, was painful and perilous, however exquisite
their pangs.

Not so today. Romantic love and falling into it is part of
the air we breathe, and marriage without it unthinkable.
Champions of sexual freedom are accused of taking all the
mystery and romance out of sex by dispensing with the solemn
ritual of courtship. A major romantic revival is being promoted to accompany the chastity, monogamy and family
values which are being urged on the population in this Post-
AIDS era. The "hype" shows every sign – increased sales
of Valentine tokens being but one – of runaway success.

As one whose childhood memories are saturated with the
June moons and blushing heroines of popular 1950s romance,
my own heart rebels against romantic revivalism. What I
remember is the political retrenchment of those never-had-it-
so-good post-war years; the rigid class boundaries, our
mothers" retreat into domesticity (and a like fate being

assumed for us their daughters by the Cookery Mistress and the Minister of Education). For many of us this new version is little more than a sprinkling of sugar, and a pretty cloying, synthetic-tasting sugar at that, on the pill of a bleak new sexual conservatism.

The Church's interest in all this is apparent and inevitable in the light of its enormous investment in the institution of marriage. The common consensus of Church teaching on marriage is that it does not derive from faith in Christ but is "originated in nature and society"[1] which immediately raises the problem of defining what we mean by these terms. Social pragmatism has a way of passing itself off as "nature", as does popular sentiment. So we have to ask whether the Church's interest in the social institution of marriage necessitates a corresponding investment in the social ideology of the "new" monogamous morality. If so, how is it to avoid being "conformed to the world" – to its present conservative trends in particular, and perhaps even more importantly to the emotional perceptions of late twentieth-century consumer culture. How, furthermore, is the Church to uphold the permanence of marriages in which love as we see it has failed and faded – as it does? Love's transience is all part of the story, as all the songs and the one-in-three marriages that end in divorce tell us.

Non-attenders, and in many cases non-believers, ask to be married in church because they wish to pledge their love in more awesome language than the secular world lays on for these occasions; they want the something extra, richer and deeper that a Christian liturgy uniquely provides. I do not think Christians, clergy or laity, should be snobbish or sectarian about this. "Falling in love", if that is how people name the trust and recognition of one another on which a life-long union can be contemplated, is an ineffable, other worldly experience, perhaps for many the first apprehension of eternity, of something "bigger than both of us". It is during preparation for marriage that many people nowadays first come into contact with the faith. ·

Christian marriage is officially taught as a distinct and separate undertaking from marriage in "the world". While a church wedding is granted, as is a state (register office) ceremony, on the basis of the couple's intent to form a life-long union, the Church departs from the state's function in so far as the Christian sacrament only "takes" when the marriage is consummated and, together with the solemn promise to "forsake all other" consummation, serves as a bodily sign of a holy mystery in which man and woman become one flesh. They form not a new social unit, but a new body in *the* body, the Church. In that sense Christian marriage remains far more earth-bound than feelings-bound.

It seems to me a·matter of considerable urgency at present for the Church to stress the distance between its marital theology and popular sentiment – just as it needs to distance its vision of justice from market force economics – and one of the most effective and honest ways it can do this is to acknowledge its own troubled, contradictory history in these matters.

As we saw in chapter 3 the medieval Church's disinterest in conjugal sentiment was near absolute. Its basis in nature was recognized but this was more a matter of sorrow than celebration: something to be kept in check; as could be seen in the celibate clergy's prurient interest in couples' sex lives. During most of this period marriage was purely a matter for society. All matches were social investments of one sort or another and the commercial and dynastic interests of the upper-classes were constantly changing. "When the alliance which had answered would answer no longer, the husband's object was to get rid of the lady as quickly as possible. Many marriages were dissolved."[2] With marriage held in such low esteem it is not surprising that, until the thirteenth century, the Church in general maintained a *laissez-faire* cynicism towards these transactions. Despite the considerable efforts of individual reforming Popes and pastors to check abuses and to bring marriage under the Church's wing it was not until the Council of Trent in 1538 that a Christian ceremony was considered essential for a proper marriage.[3]

The elevation of the spiritual and social status of marriage was a *cause célèbre* of the Protestant revolution in the late fifteenth and early sixteenth centuries. The debate about love and marriage in the Renaissance world was largely conducted in sectarian terms and my primary purpose in this chapter is to challenge the limitations these terms have imposed on our imagination. There is, however, one important point that I wish to stress at the outset. While I argue, here and in chapter 3, that the celibate system devalued sexual love, and moreover that it actually reversed the long cultural/ethical process towards a juxtaposition of love and marriage, we have to qualify what we mean by love. When Shakespeare writes about the "course of true love" not running smoothly he did not mean what St Paul meant by love in marriage. "True love" as such was not invented until the twelfth century so we can hardly accuse the early Church of perversely land-mining its path! Whether the troubadours invented, redis-covered or were merely the first to give voice to this "new" sentiment is something we cannot know. However, as C. S. Lewis wrote:

> There can be no mistake about the novelty of romantic love, our only difficulty is to imagine in all its barrenness the mental world that existed before its coming – to wipe out of our minds, for a moment, nearly all that makes the food both of modern sentimentality and of modern cyni-cism. We must conceive of a world emptied of that ideal of "happiness" – a happiness grounded on successful romantic love which still supplies the motive of our popular fiction.[4]

The early troubadours did not delude themselves with hopes of happiness. Some took their cue from the worldly-wise Ovid for whom love was a minor peccadillo of life and the joke of his *Art of Love* lay in pretending to take it seriously. Others, though, according to Lewis, fatally mistook Ovid's purpose and languished away in hopeless passion. The Church's genius for spiritualizing the new feeling has been noted and one can only hope it gave comfort.

Héloïse, as we know, refused the Church's consolation for the pangs of her betrayed and mispriz'd love. The general impression left on the medieval mind that sexual love (which included, we should remember, "excessive" warmth between spouses) was wicked, produced in poets like Chaucer a "readiness to emphasize rather than to conceal the antagonism between their amatory and their religious ideals".[5]

St Bernard did not have the last or the only word to "the world" or indeed to the cloister for whom he framed his meditations. Marina Warner describes the ways whereby ascetic religious fervour became deeply intertwined with the ritualistic postures of courtly love. Hell-fearing asceticism was itself softened in the middle and later medieval period and these new sweeter strains of Christian piety stressing the humanity and self-giving love of Jesus was, says Warner:

> often close in *terminology* to *le gay saber* of the Troubadours, though as distant in *meaning* as the fables of China. Chivalry and asceticism were also related in their cult of suffering and self-sacrifice – the lover's discipline on behalf of his lady was easily transmuted into the ancient Christian ideal of self-martyrdom, although the psychological aim of the two is distinct.[6]

In Ovid's world martyrdom to love was always seen as insanely self-destructive, a thing which maidens and men pleaded to their gods to be delivered from. Not so for medieval

Christians. This was also a period of intense missionary zeal and one by-product of renewed ecclesiastical activity in France was the indoctrination of local poets in the rigours of Christianity's sex ethics which were always, albeit without great enthusiasm or commitment, upheld in theory, and so this teaching could be brought into the service of poetic ideals of love and honour.

Courtly love, with its tortuous ritual and its celebration of adultery, seems as distant to us as the fables of China. Except for one thing: it saw and sought *emotional* parity as the hallmark of true passion. The Lover's claim to spiritual integrity lay in his single-minded devotion and absolute fidelity to the Beloved. The social *raison d'être* of medieval romance was the feudal marriage of convenience in which the possibility of constancy based on passion of any kind, bar possibly the consolatory love of honour and kin, was remote. As the system broke down so too did the perception that *only* outside marriage could True Love be found. Romance-as-adultery became discredited and a new ideal was not only possible but necessary: spiritually, socially and ethically.

By the late fifteenth century romantic love was an ideal whose time had clearly come and the Church had to move from co-option to real accommodation. Courtly love was transformed from the Romance of adultery into a purified, Christianized but equally romantic and lyrical quest for a True Love whose proper end and meaning rests in monogamous marriage. The new ideal was forged in the new world of the Renaissance. Sweeping political and social changes enabled ideas to spread and fuse more effectively than ever before. The newly powerful nation states gathered feudal fiefs of nobles, small kingdoms and monastic realms under their rule and this gave rise to wider concepts of citizenship and societal values and rights which in turn fed the hunger for Reform both in society and in the Church, where abuses of the celibate system had become common[7]. The protest came from both sides of the cloister wall: from monks like Luther for whom the imposition of clerical celibacy was but one symbol of a defective doctrine of grace, and from an upright German citizenry angry with priestly seducers of its daughters. Everywhere increased literacy and the development of printing processes removed the cloister's monopoly of learning and, ultimately, its exclusive guardianship of moral values. Piety, released from its enclosure in monastic chastity, could now be pursued through civic duty, in marriage and begetting.

Both sides of the Reformation/Counter Reformation conflict, as it has unfolded to the present day, claim the highest and best Renaissance ideas for their own tradition. The area of sexual values is the battleground on which each side has been most eager to raise its colours.

I was raised under the Reformed flag with a version of events that is arguably more entrenched in the British Isles than elsewhere in Europe. The picture here is one of new light suffusing the old darkness; particularly the primitive darkness that clung around the "cattle shed" of Roman Catholic marital theory. I fell passionately in love with sixteenth century poetry, and reading only English literature I concurred in the claims of critics like Lewis that the highest expression of this "new deal" was to be found in the Puritan poets and divines: in Spenser and Chapman who succeeded most completely in reconciling Courtesy and Piety, divine and human love. Lewis actually proposes that this "if once understood explains many things in the history of sentiment, noticeable to the present day between the Catholic and Protestant parts of Europe"[8]

The idea that North European culture became – and continues to be – the repository of the most elevated sexual values is neither useful nor tenable. By focusing on women's place in times of shifting values and turbulent social change, feminism has played a crucial part in challenging the sectarian and cultural biases which have obscured our understanding of this and all other periods.

It seems appropriate and just to look to Lewis' work to identify the major flaw in the "darkness to light" theory. Lewis was a formidable scholar of European medieval and Renaissance literature whose work on the old Romantic tradition, *The Allegory of Love*, is a major classic. He is also the most popular Christian apologist of the twentieth century. The error, or the enormous logical leap Lewis takes, is a common one. He assumes that in revaluing marriage and practising it themselves the Reformers restored women to full spiritual and social dignity. Lewis cites Martin Luther's repeated praise of women, contrasting his geniality and optimism to the grim impositions of penance and purgatory that characterized the Roman attitude to the marriage bed. Again and again, particularly in his later work when charges of religious sexism had begun to be systematically laid against both Catholic and Reformed church practice, Lewis used such arguments to refute any notion that women were not well served in his own Anglican establishment.[9]

A thinker like C. S. Lewis would never succumb to bigoted anti-Catholicism in matters of "serious" doctrine or to crude insularity in his literary scholarship; but he clearly does so when he discusses marriage and the position of women, because he does not question the validity of an all-male cultural perspective in which women's value is defined by men: which the Reformers were as much given to doing as their benighted predecessors.

The genial Luther's praise of women is in fact staggeringly and blatantly androcentric. When he rails at the old Church for "denying us marriage" it soon becomes clear that the "us" is a male us, for he could match the most misogynist monk in his certainties on women's place in his world. A denial of women's moral and matrimonial worth is evident throughout Luther's proclamations: "A woman is not fully master of herself. God fashioned her body so that she would be with a man".[10] Eve's desire and Adam's rule shackled together once again! As for the honourable estate of matrimony, which was her proper destiny, it was an "emergency hospital for the ill of human drives".[11] Luther replaced the idealized virgin with the ideal housewife and when he and his fellow Reformers stressed the "mutual society help and comfort" function of marriage they leave us in little doubt as to whose comfort must be served first!

The Reformation's renewed emphasis on Scripture was somewhat selective. It is significant, though not surprising in view of the New Testament's ambiguity towards marriage as *the* model of holy living, that it was mainly to the Old Testament that the Reformers turned for biblical inspiration: to the "first marriage in Eden" blessed by God, to the quiverful of progeny by which God's favour was shown forth to the patriarchs of old. Despite the dearth of examples of conjugal rectitude among these patriarchs there was no shortage of Proverbial exhortation to "rejoice in the wife of thy youth". However robust its defence of sex and family life, the Old Testament is not without ambiguity towards women. Through its pervasive rejection of medieval Catholic culture Protestant theology revived the ancient split between the Good Wife and the Beloved. Luther's statements do not go very far towards restoring the New Testament's teaching of marriage as a holy mystery, and the Reformation as a whole failed to reclaim the diversity of vocations that the early Church sought to affirm. Paul's "household codes", rather than his more challenging teachings about the place of marriage and the nature of the family, became the definitive texts of the New Model marriage.

Women, including Christian women, now see this role of honourable matron as defective both in itself and because of the ways it was – and continues to be – imposed under Protestant ideology.

The Reformation did not just reject the requirement of clerical celibacy, it swept away monasticism altogether. The original function of celibacy as a lay tradition of holiness was not (as it doubtless needed to be) purged of abuse, but abandoned altogether. The exactions of Cromwell and his like in closing or destroying the monastic houses inflicted a particular damage on women, whose choices of life style and occupation and whose access to education have always been more restricted than those of their male counterparts. It could be said that the only really "new" role Protestantism opened up for women was that of the clergy wife! (Those so honoured have a tale of their own to tell of which I among others have written already and do not propose to repeat here.) The dispossession removed an important sphere and symbol of female autonomy, which, as suggested in chapter 3, the clerical hierarchy had never quite managed to control as it wished.

The history and the present-day experience of the women's movement have taught us the value of "women only" spaces; particularly during times of change and turmoil, which is when they tend to arise. Important spiritual and social insights have, to draw on an example from my own experience, come out of the Greenham Peace Camp. The female religious orders continue an ancient tradition in providing a specific model of sisterhood-in-struggle which today spearheads feminists' challenge to the churches.[12]

So what, in the light of these qualifications, did Reformation theology offer to fill what was clearly a vacuum? First and obviously the desirability of sexual *pleasure* in marriage: an idea of marriage founded on a meeting of hearts and minds as well as bodies. They taught the faithful that loving sexual congress was good in itself and did not need to be justified by desire of issue; that the home should and could be a site of holiness. All this gave an expanded relational significance to the Seventh Commandment. Though woe betide those who broke it. Adulterous wives were subject to the death penalty in Calvin's Geneva. The Reformers were not satisfied with cleaning up the feudal cattle-shed of casual divorce, they re-established Jesus' teaching of indissolubility with a vengeance and little reference to St Paul.[13] There is something of an irony in this since one rather famous divorce loomed large in the establishment of Anglicanism!

While we rightly look askance on claims that women's status was automatically raised by being taken to wife by virtuous divines, those same divines, requiring their children to be raised in the fear and nurture of the Lord, entrusted this function to their wives, thus ending centuries of prejudice against women's capacity as educators. To this end they added their considerable weight to the pressure, built up throughout the Renaissance period, for women's own education. Neither Renaissance nor Reformed idealism envisaged the end of arranged marriages but the new emphasis on lay holiness, the higher dignity accorded to the matrimonial state and the wife's role as companion to her husband were conducive to a more liberal attitude in this regard.

As the new ideology of marriage was lived out in the late sixteenth and early seventeenth centuries new contradictions arose to overshadow the geniality and optimism of earlier affirmation. The passionate religious politics of this period, which continued well into the eighteenth century, had an important effect on the marital theory and practice of the various factions. The Puritan party vigorously upheld woman's new place of honour in the family as well as her participation in the priesthood of all believers. "Spiritually the woman, like the man ... must pursue her own salvation as an individual, even if it conflicts between husband or authorities. However Puritans only recognised the legitimacy of this conflict *vis-à-vis* Catholic or Anglican husbands, not those of the true or Reformed tradition"[14] (of which Anglicanism came to be seen as a corrupted form). The Puritan husband, like the minister or magistrate, must be recognized as the ordained instrument of God's will; to rebel against him was to rebel against God. Rebellion

E

becomes heresy at times of great tension and conflict and heresy is close to the diabolical ... The witch-hunts which broke out in Europe and the New World show us that Protestantism had failed to overcome either the sexist bias of biblical patriarchy or the medieval ascetics' fear and denigration of female sexuality, for both were explosively reconnected in a renewed identification of female carnality with the demonic. Female virtue and safety lay in submissiveness, as female historians have been at pains to point out. Here, focusing upon marriage and monogamy, I would point to the sad contrast between this submissiveness *in marriage*, now the only real safe place for women – as so many widows, old independent and single women realized to their peril – and the mutuality of constancy which the Reformers claim to have restored.

The requirements of wifely obedience took more benign forms in calmer periods but conservative Protestantism continues, to this day, to absolutize the more cautious elements of New Testament teaching. So long as we refuse to recognize and challenge this selectivity we will fail to recover an ideal of love based on true mutuality or a vision of sexual fidelity which is not subsumed into family chauvinism and pale, wifely obedience.

The triumphalism with which the Reformation cause was and continues to be argued has led to a serious and damaging blindness. In undercutting the Reformation's claims to have "resolved" the dualisms of medieval Christianity, feminist theologians have highlighted a pernicious tendency of Christian thought to project on to the past all the unease and injustice in the present order. As Christianity claims to supersede Judaism, so each new church sees itself as superseding the parent Church as "the church of the spirit and faith over the old church of dead letter and rote ritual".[15] The events outlined above would indicate that women are most commonly the victims of this tendency. They are rarely called upon to define their own perspectives of and interest in shifting social and religious values: men name their own interests as progress and impose this definition on women, who are understood to be more "backward" and hence in need of control.

The assumption that there was no idealism in medieval marriage teaching has cut us off from theological resources which we stand in desperate need of today. Here we should recall some of the developments sketched out in chapter 3. Aquinas modified the sex-negativity of earlier Church fathers by rejecting their teaching of sex and marriage as signs of the Fall. Aquinas saw marriage as instituted at the Creation, "the time of our innocency" as the Prayer Book puts it for the purpose of fecundity which for Aquinas was still the sole purpose of marriage. Sex was redeemable as long as it could be deemed innocent, and "innocent" meant rational, without passion. In medieval consciousness the perilous nature of sexual congress lay in its irrationality, its *ligamentum rationis*, the suspension of intellectual activity; a danger that lurked within marriage as well as without. Aquinas was not condemning romantic passion, about which he probably knew little or nothing. He was in no position to comment whether it could be redeemed and sanctified by either emotional parity or by lifelong fidelity, for these ideas had not yet surfaced. He was simply telling us, as teachers are wont to do, to use our God-given intelligence in all things.

We find too that alongside the medieval belief in Reason as the habitation of God in humankind, there also evolved a belief in the pre-eminence of Justice in human relations. "Justice was in everything the pattern-word of the Middle Ages." Marriage was also redeemed "by a strong devotion towards justice; the partners had to be fair towards each other," writes Charles Williams.[16] I am less convinced than Williams that these ideals did much to neutralize the sourness of patristic misogyny. Nor would it seem that a more elevated theology – any more than elevated poetic sentiment – did much to improve the lives of ordinary people. The twin pillars of Justice and Reason were conceived and applied in ways that are to us absurdly limited and limiting; trapped in false anthropologies of male and female and, of course, hostile to sexual pleasure *per se*. (Aquinas agreed with Augustine's definition of rational, innocent sex; pre-lapsarian Man apparently "implanted his semen as a farmer sows his seed"![17]

But we do not have to return to the medieval world-view in order to overcome our own culture's blindness, which seems to be a deep-seated hostility towards the application of justice and reason to the sacred realm of Love. The old courtly lover's complaint of love-as-affliction certainly survives; think of those songs about helpless lovers with smoke in their eyes. Adrienne Rich names a

> fear that lucidity and love cannot co-exist, that political awareness and personal intensity are contradictions, that consciousness must dissolve tenderness, intimacy, loyalty ... Even the recognition that marriage is an economic institution – a recognition that was perfectly clear to our ancestors well into the nineteenth century – severely disturbs the contemporary, middle-class façade of free-choice, love and partnership.[18]

The new monogamous romance was, as has been said, a restructured version of the old. While Protestantism elevated woman as Good Wife, her origin as the Beloved, the mistress of men's hearts, is owed to the rich diversity of medieval culture.

Here though we must beware of the "darkness to light" approach. While Renaissance learning provided a vital context for expressing the values and aspirations of the secular world as it broke free from the restraints of theocracy, it was not an unmixed blessing. The classicism that penetrated Renaissance thought was itself steeped in the dualisms that the Church fathers themselves had absorbed from ancient writers. Classical symbolism made its first and most influential reappearance in European thought through the dialogues of Plato. The Platonic concept of a ladder upon which the soul ascends to perfection was adopted by the Christian love poets of the later Middle Ages, most notably by Petrarch (in the fourteenth century). Petrarch owes more to St Bernard's spiritualizing sublimations than does Dante, who was in fact Bernard's contemporary and pupil. Marina Warner contrasts Dante's more old-fashioned "solid, even cautious" Mariology with that of Petrarch barely a century later:

> Petrarch's Laura is ... often paired with Dante's Beatrice, but Petrarch's deepening faith and his increased reading in the Christian philosophers ... inspired him to retract his claim that love of a fellow creature could pitch the mind from the mundane to the sublime. Petrarch admits that his love for Laura deflected his will from the true pursuit of the good, and that it is blasphemy to claim at all that the love of God can be obtained by love of one of his creatures.[19]

For Dante, on the other hand, there was no such renunciation, no need to keep Beatrice in her proper place or leave her behind, "because pure love was for him pure enough to erase the line between this world and the next. ... So although Dante's exalted love of Beatrice depended on chastity, this aspect acquired a *disproportionate* [italics mine] importance in the concept of earthly love after him."[20]

Of all the medievals, Petrarch's mellifluous verse has exercised the most marked and lasting influence on the love lyric. What then do we make of the claim put forward by Lewis and others that the poetic expressions of Reformed, monogamous romance actually healed the deeper spiritualistic dualism of the old dispensation? The Reformers seemed to have adopted in no uncertain terms the Petrarchan equation of

117

purity with passivity, female passivity.

Despite the very different spiritual world they inhabited, it is poets like Dante and Petrarch, struggling to reconcile human and divine love through singleness and purity of heart, that have burnt most brightly down the ages. Germaine Greer, who holds no brief for monogamy or Christian thought, attributes Petrarch's enduring influence and stature to his passionate fidelity for his beloved. By bearing his love for Laura "conscientiously all his life he made it his salvation. In almost every sonnet Petrarch achieves a reconciliation between his joy and his pain, his body and his soul".[21] Petrarch, however, was a genius of rare virtue and for less scrupulous men in the New Age, "Petrarchism became a refinement of adulterous sensuality", in a way Dante's verse never could.

By focusing simultaneously on both forms of dualism – the sexist and spiritualistic – feminist literary criticism has developed some fresh approaches to these themes. Scholars like Warner and Greer, though widely divergent both in the material they use and in their approaches to it, consistently stress the Beloved's construction within history, so linking – far more closely than traditional scholarship has succeeded in doing – the intensely private world of poetic inspiration to the changing religious and social values of the public world.

The new dispensation called for a vision of love which could preserve and sustain the salvific dynamic of the older form; a Beloved who could point the lover to God as spiritual guide and earthly companion, but who was not inaccessible by marriage to another; or dead; or both, like Laura and Beatrice.

For a time it seemed to achieve this end. The poetry I fell in love with still moves me beyond words. Our poetic heritage would be unimaginably impoverished without the English love lyric: its roots lie deep in the medieval past but its flowering undoubtedly belongs to the sixteenth century. We may grieve, I do, that so few women love-poets' work survives in print; but some is being recovered. We can take heart from the present day popularity of a writer like the learned Christine de Pisane (fifteenth century) who combined her vigorous campaign for women's education with extolling the goodness and delight of the marriage bed. As more and more such voices speak to us from our past, we begin to hear the woman who loves and makes poems as well as the She who inspires them. As it is, women in the sixteenth century were loved in vibrant and luminous verse:

> When love with one another so
> Interinanimates two souls,
> That after soul, which thence doth flow,
> Defects of loneliness controls.
>
> John Donne

The language of God-love and human love flowed sweetly and clearly, without abstraction or sublimation, into one another. The optimism of the new dispensation is perfectly conveyed in the simplest of Spenser's poems, Easter:

> This glorious day, deare Lord, with joy begin,
> And grant that we, for whom thou diddest die,
> Being with thy deare blood clene washt from sin,
> May live for ever in felicity.
> And that thy love we weighing worthily,
> May likewise love thee for the same againe:
> And for thy sake that all lyke deare didst buy,
> With love may one another entertain.
> So let us love, deare love, lyke as we ought,
> Love is the lesson which the Lord us taught.

It is as if the poet is waking up, if not from darkness to light at least to a braver, bolder world than the old: wider and wilder too "Oh my America, my new found Land". The Classical world unearthed by Renaissance learning yielded more than the dualities of philosophical discourse: it was full of fantasy, peopled with nymphs and knights, goddesses and gods. Spenser evokes the blessing of the entire Classical pantheon and all its train of extras for his own *Epithalamion*. All these shining ones, he writes, must bow down and "stand astonished" before his bride's

> ... sweet love and constant chastity,
> Unspotted fayth and comely womanhood,
> Regard of honour and mild modesty,
> There vertue raynes as Queen in royal throne,
> And giveth laws alone.
> The which the base affection doe obay,
> And yeeld theyr services unto her will ...

Here too constancy-in-love proved the single most powerful element in reconciling traditional Christian piety to the wider world.

The romantic tradition seems to have run its course. After four hundred years of what Lewis calls "uxorious bathos" reaction is inevitable. But it can blind us to what was creative and innovative in Romance's new Christianized form. Perhaps we have become so familiar with the idea that sexual love can, or should, be contained in monogamous marriage that we are prone to short-change the innovators who first suggested the idea.

This reaction has spilled over into some political and theological assessments of the sixteenth century. It is misleading to judge early Puritanism on the repressive theocracies and dour asceticism that it came to embody in its later respectable establishments. There was nothing respectable or smug about the "abominable heresies" of the early Quakers or the Anabaptists who sought a new equality of the sexes in their revived New Testament practice of commonism of goods. The clergy household may quite justifiably have become the butt of twentieth century comedy, but the first clergy marriages were truly scandalous affairs, neither staid nor comfortable. Luther's was denounced as an "abominable bichery" by the benign St Thomas More, and wives and husbands alike paid dearly for their defiance in public humiliation, torture, even martyrdom.

Feminists can fall into similar historical inaccuracy in our critique of uxorious romance. We sometimes over-idealize the time before marriage came in from the cold of second-class status. Medieval heiresses, noblewomen and abbesses wielded enormous power and influence through the communities over which they ruled. They were formidable, inspiring women enjoying a degree of autonomy and independence which modern society rarely offers women; far more compelling figures than the serviceable Good Wife so many were later demoted to. Spheres of female autonomy were, as has been said, havens in the storm of feudal restrictions, but they were only open to exceptional women advantaged in ways few others, including men, could ever be. Most of us were in the scullery of convent, cottage and castle and most of us, rich and poor, were "given" or "taken" in marriage with little choice in the matter and scant protection either. It was one hell of a storm!

Christendom has yet to count the total losses incurred in the battles between the old Church and the new. In setting its house in order Rome was acutely sensitive to charges of otherworldly angelism. Fantasy and faith never again roamed so freely together as they had done for Dante. The Counter-Reformers substituted Justice and Reason with the conventional matrimonial pieties of the age. The new housewifely ideal was focused on the Holy Family, which became a favourite theme of painters. "the cult of humility, understood as female submissiveness to the head of house, set the seal on the Virgin's eclipse as a matriarchal symbol"[22] and much of the power and mystery disappeared from religious art from the sixteenth century onwards.

It was the poets, not the theologians, ossified in their stances of reaction and condemnation of the old, who salvaged the treasures from the wreck of feudalism and steered them into the mainstream. For Germaine Greer, an enthusiastic specialist in his work, Shakespeare was the poet *par excellence* of the honourable estate of matrimony. "Shakespeare took up the cudgels on the side of the Reformers," she writes, "giving charm and life to their sometimes strident convictions." Of all the great poets of the period, Shakespeare, uniquely, combined imaginative lyrical splendour with a realistic presentation of life and character. Shakespeare's exposition of the love-and-marriage theme was central to his whole world-view which saw no separation between poetic love and "real life", or between private and public goodness. His championship of Reformed romanticism was revolutionary, asserts Greer, because it celebrated the values and culture of ordinary, middle- and lower-class people.These values "derived from the culture of his Warwickshire ilk and diverged significantly from the received ideas of city and court. At the core of a coherent social structure, as he saw it, lay marriage, which for Shakespeare is no mere comic convention but a crucial and complex ideal."[23]

The Taming of the Shrew contains, in Greer's view, the greatest apologia for Christian marriage ever written. Kate, in her famous end speech, pledges love to a husband who is her defender and friend. Shakespeare's concern, particularly in his comedies, was to clear away the flotsam and jetsam of the old Romance by not so gentle mockery – which we see in Romeo's shallow, postured languishing for Rosaline – but above all by giving us assertive, life-loving heroines like Juliet, Viola, Rosalind and Perdita who have "no cunning to be strange" unlike their courtly, passive counterparts. Virginia Woolf once called Shakespeare the only truly androgynous writer and it is certainly true that his place of honour lies, for his feminist audience, in his creation of courageous, lovable no-nonsense women characters. And what these "new" women offer, demand and fight tooth and nail for is requited, honourable whole-hearted love from their men:

> If that thy bent of love be honourable,
> Thy purpose marriage, send me word . . .
> And all my fortunes at thy foot I'll lay,
> And follow thee my lord throughout the world.
> (*Romeo and Juliet*. Act ll, Sc.l.)

For Shakespeare this quality of steadfastness in love is both the basis of civilized values and a tangible sign of divine grace.

> It must be remembered that while Shakespeare's concept of virtue tends to the active rather than the contemplative, his review of redemptive action is Christian. Christ, the paradigm for both men and women, redeemed humanity by suffering and dying on the cross. The Christian concept of passive heroism places a high value on endurance, which in Shakespeare's ethic is cognate with constancy and hence with truth[24]

Reading Luther and his ilk, one wonders whether the Reformers deserved such excellent PR! Shakespeare, however, demolished many of their dualistic stereotyped pieties.For him these heroic qualities of steadfastness and endurance were safeguarded by women. Male inconstancy is taken as read in Shakespeare's world, causing no great upheaval, but when women are faithless, manipulative and vacillating – as they are in the tragedies – "the world regresses to savagery". However, his worldly wisdom did not lead Shakespeare to uphold a double-standard of sexual morality: his women are too strong and self-respecting to seek marriage at any price or to continue living in a dishonourable marriage. Celibacy is a viable option for the Abbess in *The Comedy of Errors*, and more significantly for the headstrong Hermia of *A Midsummer Night's Dream*:

> So will I grow, so live, so die, my lord,
> Ere I will yield my virgin patent up
> Unto his lordship, whose unwished yoke
> My soul consents not to give sovereignty.
> (Act ɪ sc. i.)

Shakespeare did not, however, portray female "purity" as sexlessness; his heroines were "upfront" in their direct addresses to their lovers and many had a good fund of earthy jokes.

Shakespeare's was a far cry from contemporary conservative defences of monogamy as male protectiveness which can only be evoked by traditionally feminine behaviour. Here we have an ideal of love founded on strong sexual passion and unswerving fidelity which survives the hardship and everydayness of marriage without descending into bathos and banality. Shakespeare's "Warwickshire ilk", the countryfolk of Elizabethan England, had long made good their claim to a more robust and wholesome approach to the business of mating; a claim made good in life and literature. Poorer peoples had long been disgusted by the dynastic alliances of the feudal upper classes and among who in the consolatory obsession with romantic passion had first arisen, and they remained far less affected by the vicissitudes of the romantic tradition as it developed in later history. Affection, forbearance and good health were what was needed to survive marriage – to survive at all – among the agricultural labouring classes who made up most of the population of Shakespeare's England. As long as marriage was still seen in Shakespeare's terms as a community interest, something to be watched over by parents and kin, romantic monogamy remained unsentimental.

However, rural culture was increasingly under threat from the Enclosures of the seventeenth and eighteenth centuries which drove people off the land and broke up ancient kinship structures. Later marriage became a necessity for the apprentices of the growing urban centres, thus stemming the traditional course of true love by removing the cultural integrity of those who had largely inspired the new.

Ideal social histories do not by and large relate their data to the emotional and sexual perceptions of their subjects. Indeed the whole field of study arose in opposition to the dynastied, private lives view of history. Feminist historians have a particular interest in challenging this separation of interests and seeking a more integrated approach. Realizing that women's place has been defined by men, their lovability documented by men, we have to work with the more abstract poetic images since in some sense they are all we have. Until recently women were, inevitably, "also rans" in assessments of social change: so asking what, in all likelihood, *she* would have been *doing* – which was considerably more than hanging around waiting for a husband – we come to a wider understanding of interaction between art and society.

The picture that emerges from a republished study by the Quaker historian Alice Clark[25] is one of women more active in production in the early seventeenth century than in the twentieth. Men were more active in "home life". Clark's central thesis is that both sexes "led more balanced and richer lives in pre-industrial society and that this had provided a better environment for the spiritual welfare of children". Clark's picture is not a rosy one. Life was tough, not everybody prospered but the hardships of the poor after the Enclosures and the removal of production from the home-based unit constituted a different order of poverty whose consequences for women were dire. Clark records the oppression and demoralization of women which arose under capitalist economy. Men and women were forced into the wage labour market. Specialized training, which had been unnecessary in home-based industry, where the relevant skills were passed on automatically, was now essential for a decent subsistence wage and largely unobtainable for women. These developments inaugurated the modern era of female economic dependence, which for radical social critics continues to form the basis of women's oppression in society as a whole.

It must be noted that not all historians take this view of history. Others maintain that industrialisation enhanced the dignity of marriage by providing a family wage for the man and making "home" a restful haven of family intimacy. This latter view, which the churches have on the whole preferred and pursued, has come to form the basis of Reformist social doctrines and of course of the pro-family values we hear so much about today.

This is not the place to argue the case for Radical versus Reformist politics, but rather to ask what bearing these far-reaching economic changes have on the Christian understanding of marriage as based "in nature and society". It seems to me crucial that we recognize how fully the whole context of marriage was altered under Western industrialism. The demise of the stem family and the consequent "privatization" of marriage was to have the most profound effect both on the position of women in society and on the state of marital ideology. A Church which has steadfastly refused to relinquish its male-centred social perceptions, or, if it has engaged in "the woman question" at all, has not seen much further than feminism's Reformist face, is ill-equipped to assess or assert its own teachings in the light of important social change. It lacks, in other words, a truly *incarnational* understanding of ethics. When marriage was revived as a social and spiritual "good" it was, at least in theory, affirmative of sexual equality. The biblical motif of the first marriage, like the poetry of the late Renaissance period at its best, spoke the language of co-operation and co-creation between humanity and God and between men and women. As long as Adam delves and Eve spins, their true love remains rooted in reality.

Literary treatment of the romantic theme underwent a great sea-change in the bourgeois culture that arose under modern capitalism. Romance's inspirational base in "village wooing" lost force in the decline of rural culture, and love literature was once again in the hands of an élite, reflecting its own values and preoccupations. The social realism of earlier celebration was overlaid with the more sophisticated eroticism and the heightened expectations of connubial bliss among the new middle classes. Here wives were the chief consumers of, not co-workers in, their husbands prosperity and were chosen chiefly as decorative, erotic status symbols. As propounded by Shakespeare and his contemporaries love and marriage was a developing argument and not yet an escapist theme. But it became so in Shakespeare's own lifetime, as Greer points out in her scathing critique of "The middle class myth of love and marriage". By the end of the sixteenth century, love and marriage romance became a major theme of a totally new genre of romantic situation comedy in which the wedding uniformly provides the Happy Ending. These plays all presuppose the sexual fidelity of true lovers after marriage but do not attempt to explore the hows or whys. How could they? There is simply nowhere to go and nothing to do after the Happy Ending.

When this happens marriage ceases to be seen as a prologue to a life of shared endeavour and the Christian ideal of marriage as the beginning of a journey, and marital harmony and constancy as arts to be learned are both undermined. In spiritual terms the teaching of marriage as a road to salvation gives way to the static idea of marriage as a means of salvation. And that is apostasy.

It has been well said that what makes its first appearance as high tragedy makes its return as farce. Romantic comedy soon gave way to farce – a form discussed in chapter 5. I want to say here, though, that I do not think there is anything "wrong" with farce: the best farces are a truthful and useful vehicle of social satire but the values and mores they deal with are those of the upper and middle classes. We are back where we started in the old Romance, with the rituals and obsessions of an élite, only now in a completely secularized form. Spiritually and theologically too we are back where we started – on the old pendulum of Eros and agape. Passion and order.

The Church has accommodated all too well to the trivialization of the erotic. It has allowed one of its most sacred ideals, the one flesh fidelity of men and women, "instituted in Eden", to be brought into the service of consumerism and status quo sexual polity. We have absolutized the social form of the nuclear family and defended it as natural when it clearly is not. (How often do we hear arguments from "nature", that is *she* has the babies, collapsed into social status quo defences of women's domestic enclosure?)

Christian thought has to absorb the important differences between a marital partnership lived out in a shared working life and one based in private emotion, between marriages rooted in the mutual inter-dependence of earlier periods and marriages predicated upon female dependency. Feminists insist that such inequality is the worm in the apple of love. I would add that fidelity to a meal ticket, however beloved and trusted, is much further down the road to compromise than fidelity to a truly mutual enterprise. If the Church continues to show greater interest in "upholding" the institution of marriage than in creating conditions conducive to its integrity the future of Christian marriage is bleak.

"By virtue of the incarnation Eros and Agape are no longer divided," wrote Charles Williams, our own century's greatest romantic,[26] "though they may be again the next moment." It is of no use to us in our present moment to heal the divide by bringing back into fashion a sentiment that has been pulled, unrecognizably, out of shape. By secularism, yes, but also by sloth and sin, above all the sin of sexism. "The grand pattern of the real glory takes long to explore and involves many opposite experiences, including boredom. It too as in

Dante leads to politics and the City..." Christians have nothing to fear from boredom, ordinariness and anti-climax, in love or politics. And if we wish to recover an ideal of love that is constant, passionate, brave and just we will have to begin to explore some of these "many opposite experiences".

F

5

The Rationalist Challenge

'Tis the perception of the
beautiful,
A fine extension of the faculties,
Platonic, universal,
wonderful,

Drawn from the stars and
filtered through
the skies
Without which life would
be extremely dull.

Lord Byron. *Don Juan, Canto II*

But most thro' midnight streets I hear
How the youthful Harlot's curse
Blasts the new born Infants tear,
And blights with plagues the Marriage hearse.

William Blake. *London*

At the end of *Twelfth Night* Malvolio, steward of the household, swears to be "reveng'd on the whole pack of you". And so he was. Malvolio's most hated enemy, the clown, was driven from court and stage. Fifty years later the Puritans had closed all the theatres and rung down the curtain on the "silly songs" chanted by free maids dallying

"with the innocence of love
Like the Old Age."

Veronica Wedgewood, one of its most eminent historians,

describes the seventeenth century as a period of bewilderment and disillusion falling between the "phenomenal precocity" of the Elizabethan Age and the "intellectual serenity" of the eighteenth century. The Old Age had created "false expectations" in its heirs, she writes.[1] One of its greatest legacies, the positive affirmation of marriage which Shakespeare gave us in his comedies fell prey, as we saw in the last chapter, to a whole series of social, economic and cultural changes. These changes continued at an ever-increasing rate over the next three hundred years, and so, inevitably, did society's practice and perception of marriage.

However much they might have dissapproved of his clowns and silly songs, the first Puritans upheld Shakespeare's intimation that strong and loving marriages were founded on affection, good humour and endurance. Even those who had chosen marriage wisely and lived it holily were sore beset in all the political conflicts of the seventeenth century. As Wedgewood points out, the poet Lovelace's Althea, of the bright gaze and tangled hair, was probably a panic stricken wife with a pile of unpaid bills, since the poet was in prison and likely, along with hundreds of others, to remain there. Many pious and loving families found themseves torn in two by the Civil War.

"Poor greenheads" was the Puritan's name for those who, having married purely for "love", were doomed to repent at leisure. Shakespeare's lovers and lasses had indeed created false expectations in those who inherited their bright hopes without either their earthy realism or the relative stability and cohesiveness of their society. (To be fair to the Puritans the theatres they closed down were far more likely to have been playing the escapist Romances and brittle comedy which burst forth in the early Stewart era, than Shakespeare.)

The wisest and best of that turbulent society knew well that life does not match up to such literature and sought to inject a dose of realism into the "happy ever after" theme.

They that enter into the state of marriage cast a die of the greatest contingency, and yet of the greatest interest in the world, next to the last throw for eternity. Life or death, felicity or a lasting sorrow, are in the power of marriage. As very fool is he that chooses for beauty principally: whose eyes are witty and whose soul is sensual: it is an ill band of affections to tie two hearts together by a little thread of red and white: and they can love no longer but until the next ague comes; and they are fond of each other but at the chance of fancy, or the small pox, or child-bearing, or care, or time, or anything that can destroy a pretty flower.[2]

So wrote Bishop Jeremy Taylor whose discourses on Friendship and Marriage represent the high water mark of Protestant idealism. The following passage reminds us how new, still only a century old when he was writing, was the claim that marriage could be compatible with the holy living to which divines like himself were called.

The stags in the Greek epigram, whose knees became clogged with frozen snow upon the mountains, came down to the brooks of the valleys, hoping to thaw their joints with the waters of the stream: but there the frost overtook them, and bound them fast in ice, till the young herdsmen took them in their stranger snare. It is the unhappy chance of many men, finding many inconveniences upon the mountains of single life, they descend into the valleys of marriage to refresh their troubles; and there they enter into fetters, and are bound to sorrow by the cords of a man's, or woman's peevishness.[3]

Milton cannot have been the first or only Puritan divine to have been bound fast in the ice of marital disharmony, but he was the first to speak of it so openly and the first in Christendom formally to propose divorce on the grounds of incompatibility. He had stayed long in the mountains of singleness seeing his own youthful celibacy as a sacrificial dedication of his talents to God. Like many another true Puritan he looked to marriage for a divine completion of his life, a source of help and sympathy in his vocation as a poet. He found himself, as many another before and since, lonelier than ever in a mismatched union. In *The Doctrine and Discipline of Divorce* Milton argues that the Reformers' rigidity on the matter of divorce arose from a serious mis-interpretation of Scripture. Milton put Jesus' prohibition in Matthew 19:9 firmly back into its context of a "trick question". The purpose of Jesus' answer, wrote Milton, was not "to cut off remedy for a good man ... but to lay a bridle upon the overweening abuses of these rabbis".[4] Nobody could have believed more fervently than Milton in the spiritual dimension of marriage; he saw the sexual union of spouses as a prefiguring of heavenly life and pleaded for divorce precisely in order that God's purpose and promise might be properly fulfilled. Puritans, as their name implies, sought to purify not just hearts of men and women but the Church itself and society as a whole, and marriage for Milton "is not merely carnal coition but a human society; where that cannot reasonably be had there can be no true matrimony".[5] These matters had been managed more easily and mercifully in early societies, particularly the Greeks and Romans, as Milton, who revered the order and balance of the Classical world, cannot have failed to notice.

"No fault" divorce laws, that is, divorce on the grounds of incompatibility, were not implemented in Britain until 1971. By coming about when it did – at the end of the so called "permissive" 1960s – it has been easy to see it as a direct outcome of this period and to lump "easy divorce" together with all the other "excesses" of the age. Many Church spokesmen today speak of divorce as a "modern" evil – the start of the slippery slope towards AIDS, child abuse, juvenile delinquency and football hooliganism! Yet, as related in chapter 4, "easy divorce" had been tolerated by the Church in feudal times, hardly a period of rampant permissiveness *or* strong "pro-family" feeling! "So wild and ungoverned a race does superstition run us, from one extreme of abused liberty unto the other of unmerciful restraint," wrote Milton. Milton could, of course, claim a respectable antecedent in St Paul for whom divorce was a lesser evil than marital warfare and one he deemed essential to the peace and well-being in which all Christians are called to live. St Thomas More had also included provision for divorce in his *Utopia*. More suggested, albeit guardedly, that to live "quitelye and merylye" in a second marriage was not incompatible with godly living, provided such was not undertaken, in the words of the Prayer Book, lightly or wantonly.

More was a Roman Catholic martyred for a faith which teaches an indissolublist view of marriage. Marriage, like all other sacraments according to traditional Catholic teaching, is indelible: it cannot be undone. So it is not a matter of whether a Christian should or *should not* remarry while a previous wife or husband is still living but that she (or he) *cannot*; the second sacrament simply does not "take". I can respect the logic and consistency of this within the framework of a theology which believes all sacraments to be "indelible". But we cannot pretend that this theology is unambiguously upheld by Scripture or that it has always been unanimously adhered to by Christian people of goodwill. It is, moreover, hard to reconcile the indissolublist hard line with the fundamental Christian precept of forgiveness. We do believe in all other areas of life that God grants us clean slates and second chances when we ask him to.

As well as showing that it is incorrect to impute hedonism and godless utilitarianism to all those who raise objections to Christianity's own hardness of heart, Milton and More both provide early examples of a plurality of serious theological opinion on this issue. Both too presage the "modern" liberal awareness that people cannot and should not be *legislated* into sexual virtue.

Who then may we consider Milton's successors? This is an important question to raise here since we are now entering an age in which straightforward rationally defended hedonism came to co-exist with the solemn Miltonic argument against absolute monogamy. The two are often collapsed into one another in arguments for the reinstatement of the "stable marriage norm". It is clear that most people, ancient and modern, who divorce do not do so because they are turning their backs on "family life" or denying the need for sexual morality but because they are seeking more workable forms. Similarly, there are many people who practise a high code of sexual honour, whose relationships are both faithful and committed, but who refuse the imposition of legal or, in the case of agnostics, empty religious forms on their unions.

I see in the seventeenth century the source of two streams of thought which has fed into the plurality of views we have today. One, traceable to Milton, is rational, high-minded and solemly moralistic. The second is indeed anarchic and celebrates sexual passion in the Lawrentian, Byronic mode (see above) as a "life force", anarchic and untameable.

Milton's was, of course, a plea for men within a male-centred morality. Like Calvin he clearly believed that marriage was instituted to help *man* live more comfortably. He lacked the compassionate awareness of Taylor who saw that "A woman, indeed, ventures most, for she hath no sanctuary to retire to from an evil husband." Milton probably deserves the censure heaped upon him by Robert Graves and others for his callousness towards the spoilt, frivolous young woman he married, and the censure of feminists for his notorious "He for God only, she for God in him", which so neatly sums up the apostasy implicit in Puritan "love patriarchalism". But I cannot but respect Milton's courage in sticking his neck out on such a contentious issue, and feel pity for one who was to see his writings so misunderstood: damned by his fellow Puritans and used by his enemies as an excuse for debaucheries.

Milton's political thought was made entirely redundant by the Restoration. Puritanism was never again to aspire to such political heights. Ironically some of its best instincts were suppressed in the interests of good government at the start of the Civil War. The Diggers and the Levellers were marital as well as political idealists. Their laws for a free Commonwealth – in which the "Common storehouses" of the nation's land and resources were "every man and maid's portion" – included the freedom to marry who and as one chose and neither birth nor portion should hinder the match.[6]

As the song says and every schoolchild knows, the return of Good King Charles meant golden days in which people resumed long curly hair, bright colours and the pursuit of happiness. Not true, of course. We all know that changes in human behaviour cannot be chopped up in monarchical periods. Charles II's reign did however coincide with a period of economic prosperity and the actual event of the Restoration really did, according to those who observed it, change the whole climate of public life in Britain, and not for the better. Charles II's court was the centre both of government and the civil service and the tone it set percolated much further down the social system than any royal or aristocratic antics of more recent times. John Evelyn, one of Charles' supporters, wrote of Britain's "loss of reputation by a universal neglect of the public for the love of a voluptuous sensual life". We can trace in Pepys' diaries the steady erosion of at least one civil servant's sexual and religious sensibilities.

A picture of dissemblance and dalliances, of periwigs and foppery has lived on in portraiture and in the plays which suddenly appeared at the Restoration. Restoration comedy has been despised in most succeeding ages as heartless, coarse and dull. However, it has never been entirely ignored and is enjoying something of a come-back today. In an article in the *Guardian* a group of actors, directors and critics examined the contemporary relevance of the genre. The combination of material comfort with spiritual unease that characterized the seventeenth century is also, they perceived, strikingly apparent in our own time. The parallels between the parvenu seventeenth century "rakes" and todays yuppy culture; the triumph of style over any moral centre are undeniable. "Style is so much more important than who you are, and if your style is good, then you'll survive. Obviously at the most superficial level, that's of interest to our style-addicted society." Another actor proposed the Stock Exchange as the most appropriate setting for modern productions, since the City is the closest parallel in our society to the world of Restoration comedy. For the director, the plays echo the extraordinary insecurity of the times. "It was a society in which people were continually holding their breath for fear of disintegration. The links with the present seem almost too obvious to mention."[7]

More importantly the plays reflect both compliance and rebellion with the values of the age. Passages of dialogue between the cool libertines and their elders reveal a dramatic tension between the pull of the past and the push of the present. It is possible then to see these plays not just as reactions against Puritan values but as illustrating the force those values still held. The Commonwealth had been in many important respects the "age of the common man" whose books were the Bible and *Foxe's Book of Martyrs,* the great best seller after the Bible (a poor substitute for Shakespeare perhaps but not without its own powerful inspiration). The Restoration's anti-Puritan propaganda could not imaginably have succeeded in obliterating ideas which had flourished during the Commonwealth; the primacy of individual conscience, the value of the individual, ideas which the newly literate continued to absorb from their reading matter. The roots of today's

Liberation Theology lie in the re-possession of biblical teachings and the practical and political implications they have assumed for oppressed readers. Christian socialists in Britain have traced their own roots back to the Levelling movement of the 1640s: a time when speculations on the theme of social justice were widespread throughout British society.

Before the Puritan Revolution it was generally assumed that people had to adapt to society but with it came the belief that social institutions could and should be changed to meet human needs. The Levellers' matrimonial theories proved too subversive for society at that time but given their continuing high view of marriage we might expect Puritan families to stand out against the callous commercialism which we see illustrated in the plays. I can find no statistics to prove, for example, that Puritan parents were automatically more inclined to respect their children's choices of marriage partners than their royalist High Church contemporaries. But they certainly led the way in theory: Puritan handbooks of domestic conduct from the more radical pre-war times preached against arranged marriage, not from sentimental notions of true love but on the practical ground that marriages without affection were those most likely to lead to adultery. Many aristocratic Cavalier families were persuaded to follow the Puritan lead in this matter after the Restoration period.

Market forces, however, militated against parental soft-heartedness. The rise of capitalism and the change from a land-based to a money-based economy fuelled the cynicism and commercialism we see in the plays. Getting a rich heiress – a dominant motif – became not just an acceptable pursuit but one that was increasingly likely to meet with success as, for a variety of reasons, the number of single women seeking husbands outstripped the available supply of husbands. The practice of endowing marriageable daughters intensified and the dowry rate went up dramatically. All this meant that there were more mismatched marriages and love-lorn single women about. By the middle of the eighteenth century, seventy per cent of the female population remained single all their lives. As already proposed, the moral and spiritual condition of marriage seems to decline in direct proportion to the level of choice available as to whether, and with whom, women engage in it. Women's dependence on marriage increased just as her dependence in marriage did with the loss of home industries which could give them a measure of independence. "Getting a husband" prevailed over finding a sympathetic partner, as diaries, plays and novels of the period all tell us. "I think I might be brought to endure him, and that is all a reasonable woman should expect in a husband," says Harriet in Etheredge's *The Man of Mode*. Farquar's *The Beaux's Stratagem*, a popular play of the period provides its young heroine with the happy ending of a divorce. (Milton would have disapproved of Farquar's characters' light hearted manner but he might have cheered the author's "message". Or would he, given his rigid patriarchal bias, have identified with the crusty old husband?)

Such a practical resolution of marital misery remained rare in real life: there were only 291 divorces granted in Britain between 1669 and 1850. But divorce is not the only solution to mismatched marriage. Nor was Milton's the only perception of what is conducive to human well-being. As feminist historians have shown, female resistance to the sexual status quo is a hardy plant and one given to flourish during the most inauspicious times for women: times when male ideology is most aggressive. Many women, Royalists and Republicans, had shown great bravery and resourcefulness during the Civil War; managing estates, pleading law-suits and protecting their properties from opposing forces in the absence of their husbands. Women do not always, despite men's wishful thinking to the contrary, happily go home and about their "proper" business when times became more settled, and there was more female restlessness and rebellion about at this time than the plays and portraits show.

The *Guardian* discussion referred to above throws an interesting light on the question of women's role in the seventeenth century. Referring to the obsession with "style", one of the actors suggests that "another more liberating suggestion flows from this – namely that if life becomes a series of stylised roles, then *how we act them may not be innate but acquired*" [italics mine]. And why then should women whose parts, in literature and life itself were even more insubstantial and stylized than the men's and rarely served women's emotional well-being, not simply see them for what they are, as male imposed roles, and refuse to play – or invent new parts. We do now and some began to then; pen, sword and later the "salon" where intelligent women debated politics alongside men became important "outlets" for spirited and intelligent women who resisted being defined by or dependent on marriage for their place in the world. Mary Astell was a fervent champion of women's education at a time when it was a fragile and expendable commodity in the marriage market. She declaimed the failure of Roundhead and Royalist alike to "cry liberty to poor female slaves or plead for the lawfulness of resisting a private tyranny".[8] My purpose here, though, is not to look at the exceptions who were by and large for three more centuries all privileged women, but to try and picture the lives of the rest.

For well into the nineteenth century agriculture remained the single largest source of employment for men and women, married or single. But as rural life lost its cohesiveness under the pressure of Enclosure the peasantry lost their traditional safeguards against marriage à la mode. The old songs of the country folk themselves gave way to the arcadian poesies of the urban upper classes who were by now the arbiters of popular culture.

The most solid, practical and intellectual achievement of Charles II's reign was the founding of the Royal Society of

London (for the Improving of Natural Knowledge). Scientific research advanced steadily and systematically under its auspices and the technologies engendered thereby were to transform the landscape of Britain and the lives of the inhabitants over the next 150 years. While social historians have focused considerable attention on the outcome of this process – the impact of urban industrialism on marriage and family patterns in the nineteenth century has been extensively analysed – less attention has been paid to the socio–sexual implications of its inception. The struggle between Faith and Reason which had rumbled on throughout the Renaissance world took on a new significance with the rise of secular science, bringing about, in Wedgewood's words, "a mental conflict stronger than (any) material quarrels", which now "divided the mind of the individual against itself".[9] Such a mental conflict is bound to *have* sexual implications, dramatic shifts in religious consciousness always do, although in this case they are hard to pin down.

The conflict between science and religion seems remote to the twentieth-century mind. Science has – or had until the advent of quantum physics[10] – nothing at all to say pro or con about the existence of God or the supernatural, so how can new knowledge of the workings of what is, if we choose so to believe, God's handiwork undermine faith? The split arose from the way the Church absorbed, or more accurately refused to absorb, new knowledge into its own language and symbol system. Copernicus' discovery (in 1543) of planetary movement round the sun undermined the cosmological imagery upon which much Christian language had been based. When Galileo took up (and improved upon) this theory Rome chose, because then it had the power to do so, simply to outlaw it, to condemn Galileo and to reassert the old Faustian associations of science with Devil worship. Though most early scientists (and many later ones too) were men of deep religious conviction they were forced to demand their freedom from ecclesiastical control.

There was no immediate or by any means universal retreat of faith before the advancing tide of scientific enquiry; certainly not for the mass of ordinary people who had no access to its language or its data. There was rather the loss of a common language of faith which embraces all categories of human experience. Disinherited from the spiritual implications of their work scientists developed their own language and ethic of value-free neutrality.

Still less does science pronounce on sex ethics: so how in relation to the theme of this book can a knowledge of how blood circulates round the body diminish an understanding of the body as a temple of the Holy Spirit? Yet a new note of cool detachment which pervades the sexual discourse in the late seventeenth and eighteenth centuries would suggest that such an understanding was indeed lost.

The habit of diary-keeping, and the voluminous recorded correspondence of public figures like Pepys and Boswell have furnished far more detailed information about the lives and thoughts of prominent men and their times than is available in earlier ages. A recent biography reveals, for example, that James Boswell hardly ever walked home without taking in a prostitute on the way. Such debaucheries appear completely different in flavour from the riotous abandonment we read of in the early Restoration period. A sense of rebelliously kicking over the Puritan traces gave way to a cool, gloomy matter-of-factness. Boswell, apparently torn apart by his "Christian love for his pretty young wife" and an over abundance, as he put it, of "amorous faculties", was also terrified of losing his faith through debating theology with rationalists; which seems to suggest that his mind at least was seriously divided against itself by the struggle. Other less tortured souls managed rather better to accommodate themselves to the cool sexual climate of eighteenth-century rationalism.

The climate was further sustained by further shifts in public politics. The secularization of knowledge proceeded alongside the secularization of politics and public life. Theocracy was to all intents and purposes dead; the clergy still had hell fire in their armoury but the fires of the Inquisition that had persecuted Galileo finally died away after four hundred years, as did passionate sectarian loyalties which had sent men to war and execution. Religious faith became more and more located in "private life".

In much the same way social change (outlined in chapter 4) had made marriage assume a more private place in people's lives. Middle-class wives who passed their time in gossiping and flirtation had no serious moral cause against an adulterous husband: marital harmony was moreover no longer essential to the cohesiveness of the wider community and so the bitter sex war conducted in the drawing rooms of the bourgeoisie were par for the satirist's course but of little real import to those outside their circles.

The displacement of both sex and God to the "private sector" restructured the entire framework of ethical discourse. There arose a new way of talking and thinking about the body which inevitably meant that sexual activity too acquired a new language. Exalting libertinism as an extension, fine or otherwise, of the "faculties" would have been meaningless in the old pre-Copernican world where men still saw themselves as somewhere between the angels and the brute beasts. Though many opted for cheerful animalism over bloodless angelism they knew what it was they were choosing, knew too that they were putting their souls as well as their bodies on the line. The moral redemption of the soul belonged to the Church (which had preserved respect for her virtue if not her intelligence); but the body, both in private and social dimensions, was the business of man's all conquering and ever extending mind: the faculties, amorous or otherwise, by which he would unlock the secrets of the universe.

In Descartes, a guiding force of Enlightenment thinking,

a new form of dualism appears: one which came to dominate Western culture over the three succeeding centuries. Descartes taught that being derives from thought, *cogito ergo sum*. The mind and the body were seen as separate entities, enjoying a functional but not absolute relationship to one another. (Descartes first located the soul in a particular and rather obscure gland of the body.) Descartes regarded the human body as a machine and the total quantity of motion in the world as constant, so the soul has no effect on what actually happens and there is no "real" energy that we can call spiritual energy.

Under the old Hellenistic model the body was seen as separated from the "pure" mind/spirit. Under what is called Cartesian dualism body and soul together – a new line up – are both "contingent" upon intelligence. It was Descartes who sounded the death knell on the Church's claims to moral and intellectual supremacy with his dictum that all questions concerning ethics, God or the existence of a soul "ought to be demonstrated by philosophical rather than theological argument".

Once this new dualism takes hold, then those who can (mostly and for obvious reasons men) do extend the new principle of bodily neutrality to their own sexual appetites and, like the gnostics of old, see themselves as "progressive" in doing so. The new *Zeitgeist* really seems to have provided an inoculation against sexual shame hitherto unavailable in Christian culture. As early as the mid-seventeenth century we find the good-natured Pepys humbly seeking forgiveness for his sexual adventures of his much loved wife, but not of his readers or, as he grew older, of his God. The alienation of private virtue from public honour was complete in the great monarchic symbol who dazzled and dominated France: the glories of cool, Classical reason, order and beauty were supremely personified in the polygamous Sun King Louis XIV.

The old "magical" world of revelation lived on in seventeenth century metaphysical poetry. These poets preserved and enriched a common language of faith. Theirs was a bifocal perspective in which old and new worked together. The awe-struck innocent eye of the old piety was not for them dependent on ignorance of the new world of scientific enlightenment. Vaughan, for example, who "felt through all this fleshly dress bright shoots of everlastingness", was a practising doctor. The metaphysicals represent for many of us an oasis in a fairly barren desert. But these were not the "coming men" of the "real world". Their political and professional aspirations fell victim to the harsh politics and go-getting materialism of the age and most lived in (often enforced) retirement from public life.

The tension between the pull of the past and the push of the present is most poignantly revealed in the love poetry of the seventeenth and eighteenth centuries. Unlike the dramatists and diarists who tells us of their contemporaries' manners, the poets reveal the restless inner rhythms of the heart. In the metaphysicals the old project of reconciling human and divine love continued but more tentatively now, without the bold assurance of Elizabethan times:

> And shall our Love, so far beyond
> That low and dying appetite
> And which so chaste desires unite
> Not hold in an eternal bond?
>
> Is it, because we should decline
> And wholly from our thoughts exclude
> Objects that may the sense delude
> And study only the divine?

asks Lord Herbert of Cherbury. The question of passion's reconciliation with piety looms again.

While poets like Vaughan condemned the new "black art to dispense A several sin for every sense", the "coming men" of love poetry revelled in the detatched libertinism of the age. But, unlike the earlier erotic poets like Donne, they covered naked sensuality with fine words and intricate symbolism. Here again manner prevails over matter, beauty over truth and the combination of raunchy sex and coy, sly language can be seen at its worst in the poetry of Sir John Suckling. Suckling's own life too could not have been more different to Donne's: the former was a society playboy, the latter married for love at great risk to his own career. The self-mocking manner Suckling adopts in his verse aspires to irony but amounts to little more than cold-hearted insolence to women:

> Out upon it, I have loved
> Three whole days together,
> And am like to love thee more
> if it hold fair weather.
>
> Time shall moult away his wings
> Ere he shall discover
> In the whole wide world again
> Such a constant lover.
>
> But a pox upon't, no praise
> There is due at all to me:
> Love with me had made no stay,
> Had it been any but she.
>
> Had it any been but she,
> And that very very face,
> There had been at least ere this
> A dozen dozen in her place.

Suckling and his poetic contemporaries coolly and elegantly disdained passionate endeavour whether private or public. The Shakespearean ideal of wholehearted loving marriage as a place where we can be both intelligent angels and innocent sensualists was ever an elusive one, but perhaps never more so than under the *laissez-faire* politics of the seventeenth and eighteenth centuries.

The permissiveness extended to (privileged) men was maintained by a dearth of economic and professional independence for women. Of London's female population of 475,000 at the end of the eighteenth century 70,000 were prostitutes. Even the thirty per cent of women who did find a good livelihood as wives, by their husbands' favour, lived in danger of catching venereal diseases from these same husbands, as well as the additional and considerable perils of childbearing. It can be safely said that few women could actually enjoy the easy going sexual climate.

It is important to stress here that the high cultural profile attached to sexual laxity is no indicator of how most people behaved, which was dictated, as always, by biology and economics. In her incisive, informative *Letters on Jane Austen* Fay Weldon estimates that "half the nation's women remained virgins all their lives".[11] The medical horrors attendant upon free love found no relief until the early nineteenth century and must have acted as a powerful deterrent. It is interesting to note that the "compensations" for virginity, were more likely at this period to be preached not by the Established Church, which had long ceased to provide a refuge from the humiliations of marriage, but by women themselves: Lady Mary Wortley Montague, combining sound sense with social realism, writes: "I will not say virginity is happier – but it is undoubtedly safer than any marriage. In a lottery where there are – at the lowest computation – ten thousand blanks to a prize, it is the most prudent choice not to venture."[12] To the majority who had little choice in these matters the Church, by and large, preached endurance.

The serenity of the eighteenth century was shattered before its close by the Revolution in France, and if, as I believe we must, we take the term to mean a widespread revolt against the domestication of sex, against gender oppression and sexual double-standards, by the first Sexual Revolution. The personal was made fully political by an explosion of "protest" movements, among which thrived the first widespread coherent expression of feminism based on a systematic analysis of all aspects of women's condition – economic, cultural, sexual and psychological – of which we are the proud heirs today. The conjunction of these events is undeniable and troublesome. Troublesome, because popular history has reduced the political to the Terror – ask any schoolchild to picture the Revolution and she or he will come up with tumbril and guillotine – and the personal to godless sexual anarchy; illustrated by stories of Parisian whores desecrating Notre Dame Cathedral. Making *Liberté* synonymous with libertinism is a powerful weapon in the armoury of conservative rhetoric and one that has impeded a proper understanding of the development of sexual ideas in the modern period. The most cursory knowledge of the doctrines or the individuals involved in either revolution makes a nonsense of it.

Some historians see the Revolution as the final triumph of secularism and Free Thought over primitive patriarchal religion. On one level this is perfectly valid. The whole *language* of "rights" and the political impetus towards defining and extending these rights is the product of rigorous Enlightenment enquiry into the workings of human society. Whether this could have happened if the political and intellectual stranglehold of the Church had not been loosed by secularism is anybody's guess. Eighteenth-century Establishment theology was of a markedly pre-destinarian flavour emphasizing those aspects of Scripture and tradition which appeared to support *ancien régimes* (thus drawing upon itself, quite deservedly, the searing mockery of figures like Voltaire). But the Establishment's was not the only "religious" voice. The Revolution also signalled a reaction against Voltaire's asperity and the cool tone and formal categories of Enlightenment thought itself. The spirit which animated the underclasses and brought them on to the streets was the Romantic spirit of Rousseau – the rallying cry of Liberty, Equality and Fraternity was first formulated by him, and his passionate Social Contract (1762) became "the Revolution's Bible".

Rousseau's sexual politics (which we will come to later) were absurdly reactionary. But the renewed importance he placed on "feelings", on the need for people to be "in good heart" as well as cool, sound mind; his insistence on counting the psychic as well as the social cost of capitalism all gave validity to a whole range of disparate, often conflicting, elements of popular protest, whose roots ran back deep in time.

The Revolution provided a milieu for a religious radicalism more clear-headed than Rousseau's. It revived the old Puritan idea that institutions like Church and State are not immutable; they derive their legitimacy from service to the people. Left-wing Puritans had preserved this idea just as Puritan consciousness generally had created a muted but potent counter-force to the hedonistic morally flexible Royalist culture and society. The notorious Robespierre saw himself as the champion of those who wished to live "reasonably" and affectionately, unlike the rich he condemned for their love of luxury and unbridled sensuality.

Tom Paine, author of *The Rights of Man*, which won him a place in the history of the French Revolution, was a direct heir of the Levellers' tradition. The language and ideas in the American Declaration of Independence – generally acknowledged to be an important inspiration to the French revoltionaries – was taken straight from the English Levellers 125 years earlier.

The full force of counter-revolutionary rhetoric was unloosed with singular viciousness on the heads of Paine – who narrowly escaped execution by the English – and that shameless wanton, that "impious amazon of Republican France" Mary Wollstonecraft. Her *Vindication of the Rights of Women* (1792) remains the best defence of the highly moral preoccupations of the first sexual revolutionaries. It reflects the sober theological rationalism of Wollstonecraft's Dissenting associates in England as much as the Utopian euphoria of Paris in the blissful dawn. The Rational Dissenters or Unitarians united the liberalism of Rousseau and Locke with the old democratic impulses of Puritanism. (Along with the Trinity they jettisoned the idea of original sin, eternal punishment and irrational sexual guilt.) As her biographer Claire Tomalin writes, they inspired Mary with their blend of enthusiasm and gravity and "the spirit of prudent optimism in which they were inclined to view this world and the next".[13]

Mary's *Vindication* is both Utopian and prophetic. She whole heartedly embraced the doctrine of perfectibility, believing that men would become less vicious in their behaviour to women as the circumstances of human life improved. But, like all true prophets she combines a realistic appraisal of present conditions and relationships with a radical critique of the system which sustains them. A large part of her text is given to a passionate protest against prevailing practices – farming out infants to wet-nurses and single-sex boarding schools – that had proved extremely detrimental, often lethal, to the welfare of children and family life. The early marriage and home-based economies favoured by Mary were in many ways reminiscent of those practised – and poetized – in Shakespeare's time. She despised the wild oats sowing that had become acceptable for men with the advent of postponed marriage, for it led to the callous exploitation of women and a pernicious double-standard. She extended liberal arguments for women's education beyond the polite parameters of the salon. Women's education must be geared towards releasing the untapped half of humanity's resources, not just to creating more stimulating companions for middle-class men. Women are human beings before they are sexual beings, was the core of Mary's message, and male ideology had contrived to "make mere animals of them". It is interesting to speculate on the New Testament arguments Mary might have drawn upon had she been exposed to the Bible-based thinking of radical Methodism instead of Unitarianism. But she was not and the distance between mainstream religious consciousness and the cutting edge of religious radicalism at this time is, I believe, one of the most important facts in our sexual history.

Mary placed a high value on chastity: for her it lay in loving faithfully and wholeheartedly. Her scorn for the institution of marriage did not, as her detractors claim, lead her to preach promiscuity. She had no cause to, having seen and paid the high price exacted from women for sexual activity. Indeed along with many of her contemporaries she seemed to share the Puritan assumption that women were inherently less lustful than men. That Puritanism, in some form or another, should for sound practical reasons be attractive to our foremothers is often forgotten by a generation sold on the notion of fully exploring and expressing our sexuality: an idea clearly born of twentieth-century privilege, to say nothing of twentieth-century prophylaxis. As Harriet Gilbert writes in her highly irreverent (and deliciously funny) *Woman's History of Sex*:

> Sober diligent responsible men may not be a barrel of laughs but at least as lovers, should they get you pregnant they're likely to "do the decent thing" and, as husbands, will probably refrain from excessive drinking, unprovoked violence, constant infidelity or giving you a dose of the clap. Besides which, like early Christianity, Puritanism offered strictness: an easier state of affairs for the powerless (which women still very much were) than whimsicality, moral vagueness, sudden switches in what is encouraged and what will get you into trouble.[14]

Mary's sound commonsense did not save her from the common fate. She died in childbirth and the movement she spoke for was crushed. The women's clubs, which had been the power-house of French feminism, were abolished by Robespierre in 1793, its leaders guillotined for attacking the Terror; and male supremacy in all areas of life was fully restored under the Code Napolean.

All the libertarian movements that had surfaced in revolutionary France flowed on into the nineteenth century. The French Revolution dominated the politics of the nineteenth century rather as the Russian Revolution has dominated the twentieth. It gave the world an example of the transforming power of ideas which affected all subsequent history. There were ideological and political realignments; retrenchment, reaction and compromise aplenty, some of which form the subject matter of the next section. But over, above and throughout there was an openness to new possibilities, an unstoppable energy and an earnestness in everything people did and thought which must be stressed at the outset.

By the middle of the century apparently indestructible institutions like slavery, and in some countries monarchy, crumbled and by its end monogamous marriage – and the theological, ethical and social consensus on which its practice had hitherto been based – was subjected to a bombardment of "isms": Darwinism, Marxism and Freudianism. Engels' analysis of monogamous marriage as a patriarchal construct, and his even more radical proposition that it was but "a phase" in human evolution did not come out of the blue: it was prefigured by a debate about sexual relations that had long exercised the minds of more conventional Victorians. As Kate Millet writes, "In no period of Western literature had the question of sexual politics or of women's experience within it grown so vexing and insistent as it did in this".[15]

While continuity is fully acknowledged on the political front the revolutionary fervour that seethed through early nineteenth-century England belies any notion that it had all somehow happened "over there"; continuity of ideas is denied to the world of personal relationships. These have instead been stifled in cliché. The commonest cliché employed in speaking of sexual behaviour is that of the pendulum swinging between permissiveness and repression. Queen Victoria herself is evoked as representing the "strong family values" of her time after the flaccid debaucheries of the Regency. Since we are due for a swing back to the family values of our own Queen and since repressive measures to hasten this process are undertaken on the assumption that society as a whole wants a return to "normality" after the "excesses" of recent times, it is time the pendulum theory was stripped of its spurious respectability. It just does not work for one thing; for another it has spawned a dozen more – equally inane and delusory. The very word "Victorian" has become little more than a stick for Right and Left to beat each other with.

The trivialization and distortion of the sexual debate is due in large part to the repression of the movement which had promoted and sustained it. Recovering the continuity of feminist ideas is now seen as a crucial project within the movement, because we find, even today, after 150 years of articulate visible challenge to male ideology, that "each feminist work has tended to be received as if it emerged from nowhere, as if each of us had lived and thought and worked without any historical past or contextual present"; and that each contemporary theorist is "attacked or dismissed *ad feminam* as if her politics were simply an outburst of personal bitterness or rage".[16] This destruction of history is not just bad for women's advancement, it has distorted human self-knowledge on the very issue of sexual relations, that we are most urgently trying to grapple with today.

Public debate about marriage resurfaced in the mid-century. Rationalist philosophers, such as J. S. Mill and the early (Owenite) socialists, lined up against the new Romantics. The former took up many of Wollstonecraft's arguments while the latter, notably Ruskin and William Lecky, followed by a host of Victorian poets, including Tennyson and Coventry Patmore – retorted with the cult of True Womanhood and a revival of old-fashioned chivalry (thus giving the lie to Burke who had pronounced the tradition dead with the French monarchy).

The fundamental goodness of Natural Man, proclaimed as a revolutionary doctrine by Rousseau, was applied by his followers to married women. The island paradise of Rousseau's Noble Savage became the bourgeois home over which she reigned as undisputed queen. Most sane people today see this rhetoric as both obscene and absurd in the light of the enormous gulf between Idealised Womanhood and women's real lives; and in the light of the heavy doses of artifice and flattery applied by Ruskin and his ilk to prop up the "natural" division of labour they assigned to the sexes.

It is important to realize, however, that the notion of women's superiority was a brand new one: a total reversal of earlier ideologies in which it was thought necessary for women, being morally weaker and more carnal than men, to be under male control: preferably, in pre-Reformation times, in cloistered chastity. Now, as sexually active beings – well, exactly how "sexual" they were thought to be is a matter of considerable debate – they became the guardians of men's souls and the keepers of the nation's conscience. Whether such an idea would have gained ground if women had, at this stage, spoken for themselves remains an open question, but we do know that women took up their moral crusade with a determination that was greatly to disturb those who had handed it to them.

Burke's statement that "a woman is but an animal and an animal not of the highest order" might seem sufficient condemnation of conservative gallantry. But there were others for whom the notion of chivalry was more than a self-serving cop-out. Many Victorians really did try to tackle the sexual double-standard, however contradictorily. Men were exhorted to be "pure", tender and faithful and to inculcate these values in their sons. We call this Victorian repression nowadays, but is it really so different from today's earnestly enlightened parental attempts to combat "machismo" in boy children? Childhood "innocence", indeed the whole notion of childhood, was very much a Victorian "invention". Their protection came to be seen as the central function of the family. And, of course, the strongest argument for monogamy; one which had never before been advanced on this basis. But that is not all: the idea of infant innocence and vulnerability, however sentimentally voiced, was also to provide a powerful impetus towards alleviating the barbarity with which children were treated in nineteenth-century industrialized England.

Nevertheless personal piety was seriously compromised by an unwillingness to see marriage and the family in political terms. The most minimal reforms were resisted by the Romantics. Divorce rights and property rights were seen as ignoble causes; irrelevant in a world where good men "naturally" cherish the angels in their houses.

In his *Subjection of Women* (1869) Mill launched a vigorous attack on the whole emotional and economic basis of latter-day gallantry. He dismissed the "handing over" of feelings to women as superficial cant, "an education of the sentiments rather than the understanding". If the "ideal marriage" proposed by the anti-feminists was in reality so inviting a prospect to intelligent women, why, asked Mill, had they found it necessary to close off all other options? While he never doubted monogamous marriage to be a primordial form of human society, Mill went further than other liberals of his day by challenging its androcentric character; the system whereby "two became one and that one was the man". Marriage, said Mill, was neither women's true nor only vocation. Proper educational and employment opportunities must be opened up so that they can make their own way in the world.

Mill saw that a morality based on biological determinism was no morality at all. He took up Milton's argument that a morality based on legal compulsion was equally unworthy of the name but, unlike Milton, Mill applied the principle to both sexes and pressed for more flexible civil rites of marriage. Mill's ideas and inspiration were essentially those of Classical humanism. He saw marriage, as the early Romans did, as a school for civic life which had regressed in Christian culture into a "school for despots and slaves".

It is clear to me that, had he been minded to, Mill could with profit have drawn upon a host of biblical and theological arguments in pleading his case: "blessed rather are they that hear the word of God and keep it" is one obvious example (Luke 11: 27). It is even more significant that Ruskin, who did couch his arguments in "spiritual" language, was vehement in forbidding the study of theology to women. He was suspicious of all forms of strenuous mental exercise for women but this one would, above all others, render them "unwomanly". In other words female perceptions in this field were the most disruptive of all. By and large, though, clerics and theologians when they did not ignore the debate altogether treated liberal ideas, and particularly the demand for divorce, with scorn and suspicion. Overt antagonism arose between the clerisy and the early nineteenth-century socialists, who were the first and most vociferous campaigners for marriage reform. Since a seminal tract of this movement was Robert Owen's *Marriages of the Priesthood in the Old Immoral World* (1835) the hostility is not surprising! The schemes the Owenites put forward to incarnate their sexual radicalism faltered but they nevertheless provide an important bridge between earlier Utopianism and Engels' proposal of a social revolution in which the monogamous family ceases to be the main economic unity of society.

The Owenites were among the first to advance the view that character was socially constructed, not biologically determined, and to link this perception to marital theory and politics. Owen saw three sources of disunity and strife in society: a) religion; b) marriage; c) private property. All encouraged selfishness and family chauvinism at the expense of agape. Owen set up Communities of Mutual Association based almost entirely on female emancipation, "the equalisation of knowledge, rights and wealth between the sexes and a companionate sexual philosophy", which would, Owen and his followers believed, lead to "an entire reciprocity of happiness". It is important to stress that not all Owenites believed in his social experimentation, and as Barbara Taylor, who has written an illuminating account of the movement in her *Eve and the New Jerusalem*[17] tells us, only one community's experience is documented in any detail. The "companionate sexual philosophy", however short lived, was embraced with particular enthusiasm by women, who appreciated its absence of licentiousness and its belief in the idea of "nature's chastity". The communities were places of unity of home and work, not places of "free love", although there were, inevitably, "advanced" members who tried to make them so. Tensions and economic difficulties brought the scheme to an end. More debilitating, however, was the realization that the old "immoral world" of capitalism was not the transitory, fragile form many had hoped.

Social Utopians came to pursue the more conventional means of reform. Women in the culturally dominant middle-class family became, as we have seen, a "special interest group" with their new role of purifying society. The rest constituted a "problem group" which was to become the focus of their more privileged sisters' reforming zeal.

Some facts and figures are in order here. There continued to be more women than men in Britain. In 1850 there was a surplus of 50,000 women throughout the country and by 1890 their number had swelled to a million in London and around two and a half million in the country as a whole. Enter the Genteel Spinster, who in earlier times would have found a place in the extended family, possibly the rural home of a married relative, where she could earn her keep but who was now condemned to underpaid governess posts if she was well-born enough to have received an education or, if not, or if she was old and in poor health, to semi-starvation in a shabby furnished room. Her plight, so vividly depicted by Victorian novelists from Brontë to Gissing, made a rather tasteless joke of the prevailing mythology of Womanhood. The plight of women in the new industrial underclasses, married or single, makes a sick, sad mockery of it. Clearly, chivalric ideas were not to be wasted on poor women. I can still recall my schoolgirl horror when, in studying nineteenth-century Factory Acts, I saw the gulf between labour conditions and the world of crinolined, cosseted women and masterly men I had inherited from songs, novels and Christmas cards. Of course men were brutalized as badly as women under the labour system, but as far as I can tell only recent feminist history has pointed out the full extent of the brutalization the system wrought on the relationship between them. The marriage relationship itself was callously exploited as a convenient unit of production.

In quoting the following testimony of a woman "drawer" in a Midlands coal mine Kate Millett directs the reader's attention to the position this woman occupies in relation to her connubial master as well as to the abuses perpetrated on her by her employers:

I have a belt around my waist and a chain passing between my legs ... The pit is very wet where I work, and the water comes over my clogs always, and I have seen it up to my thighs ... my clothes are wet through almost all day long. I was never ill in my life but when I was lying in. My cousin looks after my children in the daytime. I am very tired when

I get home at night; I fall asleep sometimes before I get washed. I am not so strong as I was, and cannot stand my work as well as I used to. I have drawn till I have had the skin off me; the belt and chain is worse when we are in the family way. My feller (husband) has beaten me many a time for not being ready. I was not used to it at first, and he had little patience. I have known many a man beat his drawer.[18]

Perceptive, intelligent people in the nineteenth century could not fail to notice the contradictions between Christian values and the realities of a society purportedly based on them. The marriage and family life in which these values were enshrined were not just exploited but totally denied to enslaved black people. The whole system of slavery – which had been exposed in popular literature and the extensive documentation amassed by abolitionists – operated on the denial of fatherhood to men and the destruction of any sexual bonding between black men and women. The abolition campaign had radicalized many Victorian women and when it was over they turned their attention to industrial slavery at home – an enterprise for which they had the full support of men of goodwill – and to the domestic and sexual slavery of their sisters, for which, in many cases, they did not.

Of those million "spare" women in late nineteenth-century London an estimated 80,000 were prostitutes, an increase of 10,000 over the century. The arguments by which prostitution could be accommodated to "civilized" societies are as old as the profession itself. From the time of Augustine onwards it was tolerated as a more or less evil necessity in Christian culture. Aquinas compared prostitution in cities to "a sewage system in the palace. Do away with it and the palace will become a place of filth and stink." The degradation of those who serviced the sewage system could be comfortably ignored by a Church which perceived women as temptresses and men as victims of their own "natural" lust; and later by a permissiveness which invested the "woman of pleasure" with a daring glamour.

These views were no longer sustainable by the nineteenth century. Women who took to prostitution were demonstrably not exploiting men's weakness but were themselves victims of it. The Ruined Maid – the poor girl seduced and abandoned to the streets – was more than a stock character of Victorian melodrama. She was real, there were thousands of such women and their plight was given flesh and form by Victorian novelists like Dickens and Mrs Gaskell. These books were often denounced. Mrs Gaskell's *Ruth* (1853), for example, a gentle plea for mercy towards unwed mothers, was discussed in terms of whether a gentleman would let his mother read it (in much the same way as *Lady Chatterley's Lover* was a book to be kept from "wives and servants"). But ten years later wilful ignorance of these unfortunate happenings could no longer pass itself off as refined innocence. The extensive researches undertaken by Victorian philanthropists further demonstrated beyond any doubt that poverty and the social dislocation brought about by industrialization lay at the root of what was euphemistically called "the moral question".

Venereal diseases became rife, particularly among the soldiery, and new laws, the Contagious Diseases Acts drawn up in the 1860s, led to an an enormous public outcry which brought the whole question into the public arena. In the words of Josephine Butler, who led the campaign for abolition, it "let in a floodlight" on the double-standard and on the "immorality which exists among gentlemen of the upper class".[19] The CD Acts stipulated that any woman living in areas close to military centres could be termed a "common prostitute" and forced to undergo medical examinations or serve a prison term of hard labour. The arguments for the Acts turned on the same two points on which tolerance had always rested: the need to keep the "sewer system" functioning and the assumption that as continence could not possibly be required of men, the women they "required" had to be provided and in an orderly manner.

As a feminist active in the Christian wing of the peace movement I feel passionately about the connections between militarism and sexism; but a whole book would be needed to spell them out properly. While the monogamous ideal is used to keep the soldier at the front line fighting for England, home and beauty we find that everyday military discipline and morale depends upon the orderly provision of another kind of woman, the whore.

The Victorian CD Acts led to unspeakable brutalities and as always, and everywhere from the Crimea to Cambodia, it was the most vulnerable, the very young, the poor, the homeless women who were the most severely abused. It further emerged in Butler's investigations that the brothels which the government proposed licensing in its attempts to regulate prostitution in society at large operated as centres of a flourishing white slave traffic, specializing in virgin girls and child prostitutes. This was no harmless hygienic provision for gentlemen chafing under long engagement to their virgin brides; this was nothing less than the hideous underbelly of Victorian marital propriety.

For Butler and her associates the abolition campaign was a crusade, the culmination of a lifetime's work among what one of her clerical enemies termed "a class of sinners whom she had better left to themselves". Calvinist economic thought had given further ballast to the old division between "good" wives and bad whores. Prostitutes came into the category of the "undeserving poor", their "chosen" status in life showed that they were unloved by God and there was thus no reason why they should be loved by respectable men and women. Josephine Butler is deservedly recognized as a Victorian saint but I suspect she would be uncomfortable in the hagiographical packaging which has surrounded her image. The tendency

161

to "individualize" saints is even more marked in the case of women and in Josephine's case her image has worked to isolate her from the great political movements of her time. She was a mystic – haunted by a vision of woman aspiring to heaving and being dragged back into hell – but not a lone one. Her writings, particularly her introduction to *Women's Work and Women's Culture* show her to be a socialist feminist in the best Mill–Wollstonecraft tradition. Her most loyal supporters in the crusade were working-class men. Butler and her contemporaries were no strangers to the terms in which modern feminists describe the institution of marriage in our society. Florence Nightingale was another Victorian saint who saw marriage in her society as little more than legalized prostitution: "The woman who has sold herself for an establishment, in what is she superior to those we may not name?"[20] For Butler the redemption of one class of bartered women was totally dependent on the redemption of the other – of the institution itself and society as a whole.

None of this is to deny her individual charisma, or her profound spirituality: the intensity of the prayer life which sustained Josephine's own journey through "the mouth of Hell" itself is moving and awesome. As is the courage, mental and physical, with which she pursued her God-given mission. I believe, however, that Butler's contribution to nineteenth-century reform is best assessed not in terms of her holiness and self-sacrifice but in (her own) terms of the considerable theological insights she brought to the "moral question".

Butler's own Anglican establishment had been heavily pre-occupied with the problems of factionalism, its own declining influence and the destabilizing effects of "secular" scholarship. Darwin's evolutionary theories, the new schools of biblical criticism, all challenged the authority of Scripture and undermined the faith of many a common – and uncommon – man (Ruskin was one whose faith was demolished by the attack on the Bible). Anglican pews were emptying fast and many of its best minds were going to Rome. The Church was having far too hard a time of it with the sectarian world and the Darwinist Devil to be much occupied with the flesh. It is significant that the repeal of the Acts, which stands as an impressive witness to the moral power of the churches in an era of declining influence, has received little attention from Church historians.

The Church found a renewed vigour and confidence, and a new political integrity too in the later nineteenth century. Newman and the Oxford Movement brought mystery and beauty into Christian worship. The socialism that many in the movement professed upheld the rationality of religion against the increasing irrationality of Victorian religious piety. This was an enormous advance on the earlier part of the century when Christian socialism was chiefly located in dissenting movements. But the too-long time gap between the earlier dissenting socialists and the later High Church Christian socialists alienated the latter from important sources of radical thought; from the Christian feminists like Butler and the sexual radicalism of the earlier Owenites. Its very emphasis on sacrament and ritual gave it a heavily clerical – and hence male – flavour and the main thrust of its admirable pastoral endeavours was towards protecting the dignity of marriage and family life in its "slum parishes" against the onslaughts of materialism and capitalist exploitation.

Butler's theology cut across all these ecclesiastical trends and preoccupations. She was not interested in ritual, denominationalism (her campaign was an object lesson in ecumenism), least of all in "protecting" the family. Her language was biblical, prophetic, even apocalyptic. She went to the New Testament heart of the matter of sexual relations and the family in a way that reconciled secular Utopianism with Christian belief. Hers was a synthesis we have still to recover. She was, however, canny enough to use as much "Victorian sentiment" as suited her. She paid tribute to women's "motherly" qualities and to the "complementary" role of the sexes – both fashionable liberal/reformist ideals – but which for her could operate authentically only in a revived understanding of the human family as the household of God. She had no time for the pedestal or for any idealized picture of womanhood: "if reality and the ideal are one, then the ideal becomes redundant". One thing only is needful.

Butler's biblical vision of sexual justice and social transformation was not for all – not least because Christian teaching has failed for centuries to make it accessible to people. For others the female equality and *solidaire* which Josephine took as God-given and beyond question flourished best in the clear air of secularism. Many women writers attribute the transformations of the past 150 years to the fact that the old Christian polarities of Eve and Mary, carnal and exalted womanhood, have, as Marina Warner says, "lost their power to heal or harm". I have no wish to deny this or to require my sisters to seek their sexual integrity through Christian imagery. But it is well to remember here that (as suggested in chapter 3) the most creative Christian women did not subscribe to the Church's image of them anyway. Earlier mystics like Hildegarde of Bingen had not seen her cloister as *the* place of female holiness in the terms her religious culture did. Women like Butler, against all the odds of her own time, refused to see marriage, even one as happy, complete and complementary as her own undoubtedly was, in that way either. From such resistance truth is born.

The novelist Fay Weldon has a totally different idea, "the better novels theory". We owe such improved moral awareness as we have, not to "wide sweeping social changes, waves in the body politic but the sharp focusing power of individuals...more novels and better novels read by more people in the opinion-forming ranks of society".[21]

My own excuse for indulging in "the kind of sweeping generalizations writers of non-fiction love to make", which

Weldon says, "can only be more or less true", is that I am trying to gather together forms and material that have long lain disconnected and connect them to this one theme. (Though the novel has undoubtedly furnished one of the most creative, probably the best means of exploring the meaning of monogamy, a novel just "about" it would be unreadable.) And it is precisely those "sweeping generalizations" which have, for good or ill, mostly ill, shaped marriage ideology. As Phyllis Rose writes in her study of five Victorian marriages, "the plots we choose to impose on our lives are limited and limiting. And in no area are they so banal and sterile as in that of love and marriage. Nothing else being available to our imagination we filter our experience through the Romantic clichés with which popular culture bombards us."[22]

Easy stories, whether they be the sterotypes perpetuated by Christian thought or the Romantic heroes and Happy Ever Afters which have dominated fiction since the inception of the "love novel", drive out hard ones.

Weldon's thesis takes us back to where we started this chapter, to the "false expectations" of marriage raised by, among other things, bad novels. I end with one or two random illustrations from the "hard stories" furnished by nineteenth-century novelists dealing with the contradictions of their own times. The times themselves demanded a richer, "better novel"; a new form with more space to explore the connections between private and public morality.

Though many Victorian novelists clung to the old script they are not the ones whose books have endured. There were Happy Endings but these came, as early as Jane Austen herself, from Character (as opposed to the accidents of beauty or propinquity) and only after a long process of self-searching and repentance by the hero(in)es. You got what you deserved in Austen's intensely *moral* books: if you opted for the security of an establishment she generously gave it to you, if you risked your material well-being – and the risks were considerable in her day – and bravely held out for love and compatibility, then you were so rewarded. If you committed adultery, though, as Maria did in *Mansfield Park*, you were cast in outer darkness with no tears shed over you.

The Victorians learnt to shed tears, if only for the properly penitent. But even the moral tragedies of which they were so fond came to break with old taboos. Till the mid-nineteenth century tragedy – in life and literature – was dominated by the theme of untimely death. Oceans of tears – and one of the best things about the Victorians was that they permitted "manly tears" – were shed over the loss of a beloved babe or an angel wife. Gradually, though, the death of an ill-matched marriage became a permissible subject. David Copperfield's marriage to his clinging child-wife Dora died before she did, as did Dorothea's misguided marriage to the cold, dessicated Casaubon in George Eliot's *Middlemarch*. In both these novels the hero(ine) is released by the timely death of the spouse to grow to maturity nourished by a more solidly-based matrimonial happiness: a literary cop-out unavailable to either of the authors, or with improved medicine and longer life to many of their contemporaries. In a society wrestling with the question of divorce, the need for a "second chance", something which Milton and co. had pleaded for to no avail for three hundred years, was exonerated in fiction. Longevity, if nothing else, concentrated the Victorian mind on this matter.

Gradually this began to happen to "good" characters, to heroes and heroines. When it happened to weak, flawed characters they were granted understanding and hero status too. Emma Bovary dies of a surfeit of arsenic and stale romance but she is Flaubert's heroine, albeit a tragic one. The real villain of her story is the script she chose or, as the author makes clear, was chosen for her by the society she lived in.

The point is that these stories were seen as interesting, important and instructive. It is important, whether we agree with him or not, that Tolstoy *could* write, "All happy families

The Rationalist Challenge

are alike but an unhappy family is unhappy after its own fashion", because he gives these families' lives dignity and meaning. More important still, Tolstoy *could not* write the "moral tale" he had planned around Anna the adulteress. He simply came to love her and so do we. Our hearts as well as the mind become larger and kindlier.

We have the space and freedoms now to write even better scripts for ourselves; that is, if we have not forgotten how to be heroes and heroines of our own ever more complex stories.

6

Snakes and Ladders

This also will pass. And marriage – marriage seems to me the effort to make that permanent which is in its nature transient. *Nequidquam, nequidquam,* in vain, in vain. (Helen Waddell, *Peter Abelard.*)

And Jacob was left alone, and there wrestled a man with him until the breaking of the day ... And he said, Let me go, for the day breaketh. And he said, I will not let thee go, except thou bless me. And he said unto him, What is thy name? (Gen. 32: 24 – 27)

Their life seemed to be like a snake biting its tail – Matthew's job for the sake of Susan, children, house and garden, a caravanserai. What for? Their love for each other ... If this wasn't the centre, what was? Yes, it was around this point, their love, that the whole extraordinary structure evolved. So that was the central point, the well-spring. And if one felt that it simply was not strong enough, important enough to support it all, well, whose fault was that? (Doris Lessing).[1]

Whose fault indeed? We are not short of answers, or of the theories and language in which to frame them. But those who seriously address themselves to the question agree that the family – the institution we have evolved to contain the lifelong monogamous unions required in a Christian civilization – is in trouble. Divorce figures are rising: more and more couples are "living together" before, or instead of, marriage.

Or is it perhaps that these patterns suggest rising expectations rather than declining morals? A healthy adaptation of the species to a changed, nay improved socio–sexual environment? Longer life-expectancy, higher living standards, brought about in part by smaller families and the means to bear only the children we want when and as we want them, have all contributed to higher standards of love and mutuality. Now at last we in the privileged West have space and freedom to nurture the centre, the pivot of it all, the man–woman relationship itself. And we can do so honestly and openly. The accessibility of "no fault" divorce, which only two generations ago was so scandalous and shameful that most people preferred to battle on in marital misery, has removed the stigma from failure. Lawrence Stone points out that:

> If one adopts the reasonable criteria of durability, marriages in the mid twentieth Century were more stable than at any other time in history. Indeed, it looks very much as if modern divorce is little more than a functional substitute for death. The decline of the adult mortality rate after the 17th Century, by prolonging the expected duration of marriage to unprecedented lengths, eventually forced Western society to adopt the institutional escape hatch of divorce.[2]

But to most Christians divorce is and remains sad and shameful. More than "durability" is at stake here. Divorce and legal remarriage have presented the Church with a real problem of order in its sacramental life as well as blurring the old ethical boundary between the virtuously married and the adulterers. Over and above all marital failure is a serious disruption of God's law and purpose. The centre is built to hold, to last for ever, so why doesn't it?

Christians are not the only people with an investment in marriage. Those who hold fast to other "secular" ideologies also feel passionately concerned for the viability of marriage: committed either to its survival or, in some cases, to its inevitable and hasty demise! Either way few people feel neutral about it.

Women have always had the greatest investment. As I have tried to show throughout this book, they have more often been the victims rather than the agents of changing marital theory and practice. It is only recently that women have spoken of their own sexual experience.

I opened this chapter by quoting from a story by Doris Lessing, for no better reason than that its publication in 1963, the year before I was married, marks the point at which I began to be personally engaged with the issues in this book. The changes that have occurred both in my own lifetime and in the twentieth century as a whole are so vast and breathtaking that anything I write about them is bound to be partial, fragmentary and subjective; so I may as well begin on relatively familiar territory, at the point where I came in.

Stories, sacred and secular, from the beginning of time have been the most powerful reflector of human sexual consciousness. Since the early nineteenth century fiction has provided a forum in which female experience of marriage, could, for the first time, be properly heard and heeded. We can no longer speak about marriage, in general or in the particular, as a single entity. According to the sociologist Jessie Bernard there is now a very considerable body of well-authenticated research to show that there are really two marriages, his and hers, and that they rarely coincide.[3]

Lessing, rather to her own surprise, has been very much guru for my own and succeeding generations of women. Women's experience of insubstantiality, of "nothingness" in a male-ordered world, is a recurring theme of her writing. Lessing's heroines seek to transcend this nothingness without being trapped in a compromise with prevailing mythology. We can only fully emphathize with Susan and Matthew's plight – and our own – by looking at the prevailing mythology that surrounded their marriage. "For," as George Eliot wrote a century before, "there is no creature whose inward being is so strong that it is not greatly determined by what lies outside it".[4] They are neither weak nor particularly flawed human beings; they are strong, attractive and, according to their lights, virtuous. And they really do love one another. Matthew's marriage is a quintessence of the ideal that prevailed from the seventeenth century till the 1960s. He sees his wife and his home life as a reward for the considerable labours he undergoes in maintaining them. Susan's marriage is a different one. It does not bring her self-esteem. By trying to live, as a good wife and mother should, "for others" she finds that she has come to exist through others. She seeks meaning, a "centre" to her own life: she seeks, in short, her self, the self that has been swallowed up in the roles she fulfils. She strips herself of everything that gives her value on society's terms to see what is left – and there is nothing. Susan is in every other way blessed materially and emotionally; her husband loves her enough and is "modern" (and rich) enough to buy her respite from household and maternal cares. But he cannot give her inner space, the soul space she needs, for in their world there is no language for it. (She leads Matthew to believe that she has a lover when in fact she is spending her time alone in a dingy rented room. When this cover is blown Susan, having by now offloaded all her maternal and domestic responsibilites to surrogates, escapes finally, by gassing herself.)

Betty Friedan's *Feminine Mystique*, the book that sparked off the second wave of feminism, was addressed to the Susans of the Western world, my mother's generation. This was the era when women stayed at home, had babies in the New Jerusalem of middle-class suburbia and having put the complex caravanserai together asked, is that all? The answer was, yes. And if it is not enough the fault is yours.

A real-life Susan would in all likelihood have been told to go home and get on with the job she had there instead of mooning about in such perverse self absorption. Quite possibly she would have been sent to a psychiatrist to get adjusted to her "role". However Betty Friedan's book demonstrates that there were millions of women like her, suffering from a "problem that has no name"; "forced to seek identity and self-esteem in the only channels open to her: the pursuit of sexual fulfilment, motherhood and the possession of material things. And chained to these pursuits she is stunted at a lower level of living, blocked from the realization of her higher human needs."[5] What kind of moral world is it when adultery is a more acceptable outlet than a life of one's own?

Despite its narrow, élitist focus on the cream of middle-class motherhood and its limited prescriptions – greater career opportunities for these same women – Friedan's book remains an important social document. It should be required reading for Christians concerned with the future of marriage; or for liberal-minded Christians who wish to come to grips with feminism. It was an essentially spiritual malaise that she diagnosed: brought about by conditions of "Christian marriage" in one of the most "advanced" Christian civilizations in the world.

Most important of all, Friedan raised the question whether marriage could or should be the pinnacle of feminine achievement or the repository of Christian values. Maybe the centre was not holding because the cocooned heterosexual couple plus 2 children was never meant to *be* the centre and pivot. Higher loving standards must be incarnated in community, not enclosed in the private family. The Gospel would appear to teach us just that, but in the mid-1960s it took a woman who was, with good reason, hostile to any religious orthodoxy to remind us. (I did not read much theology back in the 1960s but I have not subsequently found any sustained theological response to Friedan's best-selling book.)

Friedan's arguments were soon superseded by a more widely-focused feminism. This arose far from the suburban kitchens of middle America; in the ferment of Civil Rights activism and anti-war protest. The pill was about to come into general use, heralding the era which came to be called "permissive", presenting women with a host of new and more pressing conundra. Younger women moved on from questioning whether we should live in traditional housewifely marriages – which Jessie Bernard, Friedan and others had, by now, proved beyond doubt to be bad for our health – to asking whether marriage, or *any* kind of monogamous committed relationship to a man, might not also be detrimental to women's development.

Before we look at the ways women and men reacted to their "new" sexual freedom we should reflect on the fleeting, transitory nature of all these changes. Women's post-war retreat into domesticity lasted only a very short time. Professional opportunities in fact had been opened up to them from the late nineteenth century onwards and the "career woman" was by no means the disruptive modern phenomenon many present her as being. Susan, we could say, was unfortunate in being born in the wrong decade. Ten years earlier or later she might well have been "saved" by a fulfilling career of her own: indeed if there is a social message in Lessing's story that would be the one we'd be most likely to draw. (This history has been replicated over the past decade. In the early 1980s when unemployment was at its height mothers were urged by all manner of rhetoric to go home and take care of their children. Now that women are once again required in the labour market, renewed attention is given to creating ways and means of balancing home and work.)

The period of permissiveness might well turn out to be even more transitory. Less than twenty years elapsed between the pill and AIDS. The pill itself has turned out not to be the magical passport to sexual freedom and fulfilment we thought: it has been proved toxic, and potentially lethal. It is on precisely this possibility – the old pendulum theory – that permissiveness (and feminism) will turn out to be little more than hiccups of history – that many conservatives pin their hopes of restoring the old order. Sexual freedoms are already being eroded by clause 28, increasingly concerted efforts to reverse abortion provisions and a host of other changes. Tabloids and glossy magazines are constantly telling us that the 1990s is "the decade of monogamy". It seems to me unlikely in the extreme that monogamy will be reconstructed on the tenuous consumerist basis on which it is now being promoted: monogamy is fun, fashionable and you don't get AIDS; followed by tips on how to spice up a jaded sexual palate and even, as I read recently, to make your home "a sexier place"!

How much hope we pin on the "new monogamy" will be dictated by what kind of traditional morality and family life we are seeking to "bring back". The Victorian family, thrifty loyal and hardworking, seems to be a top favourite at the moment, but such a family was, as we have seen, a radical departure from earlier forms: it was itself a stripped down nuclear version of older, more extended kinship patterns. There is simply no way we can return to the older stem family with its home-based economies without shedding the entire superstructure of industrial capitalism.

The modern family has not only shrunk in size from its Victorian "heyday", it has shrunk in its function. Education, care of the sick and elderly have been assumed by an army of experts of the modern state. This has created the space for women, on whom these functions previously fell, to re-enter public life. The "pill revolution" of the 1960s and 1970s gave them the further freedom to define the terms on which they would engage in private life. It is important to realize that the greatest change the 1960s and 1970s brought about was an increase, albeit modest, in *women's* freedoms. The pill gave women the freedom to sow their wild oats, just as men have always done; and in many cases to find sexual fulfilment outside marriage should they so wish, again as men have, if not everywhere and always done, certainly done more extensively than women.

It is precisely women's freedoms, social and sexual, that have caused alarm and provoked the "pro-family rhetoric" we hear today. This has come primarily from the political and ecclesiastical right. For example, a conjunction of Thatcher supporters and Christians "concerned for" the family was formally proposed in the pages of the *Church Times* (March 1986). One might hope that such a conjunction would seek to alleviate the stresses that have beset families in the recent economic recession: might even perhaps campaign for the restoration of services, like public affordable nursery school provisions and geriatric care, which have placed increased burdens on women in an economy where few families can afford a "stay-home" wife, whether it is fashionable or not. But we would be disappointed. Instead the "crisis in the family" is presented as having been "caused" by working wives and left-wing councils who neglect the sacred ties which bind society together.

While feminists (and other dissidents) could be said to be guilty of playing into the hands of their enemy by allowing the right to capture the moral high ground of the debate, in fact a good deal of thought and action has always focused on family matters within the women's movement.

In the late 1960s and early 1970s feminism was far more concerned to challenge the patriarchal rhetoric of the left than that of the right. If the Soviet state had manifestly failed to implement true Marxism, how much more had it failed to make any sense of Engels. "Engels had supplied nothing but a history and economy of the patriarchal family, neglecting to investigate the mental habits it inculcates." By 1936 the party announced that since the state was "temporarily unable to take upon itself family functions it was forced to conserve the family."[6] One can only hope that now Soviet society has finally succeeded in shedding Stalinist repression it may be able to recover the more imaginative and truly radical aspects of Marxism.

The "free love" doctrines embraced by Western youth in the swinging 1960s were more than a hedonistic protest against the sexual repression of their elders. They sought to make the world itself a "sexier place". Making Love is after all gentler and healthier than making War even if it was, of itself, powerless to end the carnage in Vietnam. The movement destroyed a lot of the old shibboleths that needed destroying: women were no longer divided, as they still were during my 1950s adolescence, into good girls who did not "do it", go all the way; and bad girls who did. Sex was OK, cool, for women and men alike. But this sexual equality did not extend far beyond the bedroom. It is by now commonplace to point out that much of the impetus of present-day feminism came from young idealistic, left-wing women relegated to tea-making and typing in the student movements of the 1960s. Stokely Carmichael's unequivocal put down, "the place of women in the SNCC is prone", has passed into feminist folklore. The movement, then, was primarily a revolt of young men with female auxiliaries. And, as it turned out, the boys still wanted their old traditional accompaniment of personal commitment. As Beatrix Campbell points out, this conjunction was bound to prove problematical for women since it was "a sexual revolution that implied the separation of sex from reproduction, but that remained implicit and besides, then as now, there was no *absolute* guarantee against the risk of pregnancy".[7] Women had every reason to shun traditional forms of dependency on men but they came to see the need for some sort of defence against, or at least a recognition of "the differential effects of permissiveness on men and women". They came gradually to suspect that the revolution was really about the affirmation of young men's masculinity and promiscuity; it was indiscriminate, and their sexual object was indeterminate (as long as she was a woman).[8]

It is important to understand the extent to which 1960s free love ideology departed from the left's traditional critique of monogamy. I hestitate even to apply the term "sexual revolution" to the 1960s since I believe it properly belongs to a process begun back in the seventeenth century, which was more often than not severely critical of double-standardized sexual licence. The first (and longest) sexual revolution criticized the institution – the inward-looking monogamous nuclear family – not the ethic. It has become a dogma of Western industrial society that, as the socialist critic Raymond Williams puts it, "people are only partially knowable in and through relationships".[9] Only through the most intimate sexual and familial relations do we attempt to comprehend what lies beyond the ego/self. And we look no further: instead of a widening, unbroken circle of intimacy, "knowability" and community, we create a cut off point between "knowable relationships and an unknown, unknowable overwhelming society" and the place where civilized values can be sought and applied shrinks.

Early twentieth-century socialist feminists like Virginia Woolf were absolutely clear in their condemnation of cosy family values: "the private and the public world are inseparably connected ... the tyrannies and servilities of the one are the tyrannies and servilities of the other".[10] We have no means of overcoming either if we are stripped of the means of recognizing them in and relating to their "other" context. The withdrawal of women into private life in the 1950s had stripped them of political awareness and social responsibility. But theirs was only half of a universal regression. World politics had become almost totally "unknowable" by that time. The heroism of ordinary men and women, which had defeated Nazism was itself negated and defeated in the distinctly unheroic final solution of Hiroshima and the long Cold War which followed the cessation of hostilities. The outside world became the "rat race" and the home became the only place where human values could be conceived as workable for men and women alike.

The 1960s and 1970s "revolution" simply turned this dualism on its head by denying that private life could hold any values at all. It did nothing to restore a proper balance between private and public, nor did it change relations between the sexes, except the value placed on the relationality of sex itself. And women found themselves unable to let go of relationality. They found that the person one "does it" with is actually more important than "doing it". Many found that indiscriminate sex was not even enjoyable. When women protested by making "heavy" emotional demands on their men they were accused of being hung-up on bourgeois possessiveness. Those who just said no were told they were screwed up, frigid. "Frigidity," Campbell writes:

> we knew was a female condition, but having embraced sex nothing could be worse than having to own up to yourself being part of the female condition ... Instead we lurched into feminism with a mysterious sense of sexual disappointment, or with a strong yet untheorized sense of the mismatch between the natural order of heterosexual practice and the nature of women's desire.[11]

If it was an exclusively masculine sexuality that was being celebrated in the movement then it was time to find out what female sexuality was all about, how it might differ and how it too could be properly celebrated. The women's movement turned its attention to these questions throughout the 1970s; and to each other; to a recovery of its own history and a thoroughgoing analysis of women's oppression and silence therein. Women demanded their own separate space in which to define and act upon their own political priorities, which were nothing less than the liberation of Everywoman who was everywhere abused. Practical experience in projects like refuges for battered women and Rape Crisis Centres showed us that women's dependence in monogamous marriage was not just psychologically unhealthy and politically undesirable, it was literally life-threatening. Feminists all over the country saw women who were regularly and brutally beaten by their seemingly ordinary, polite husbands. If rapists were the shock troops of patriarchy, then wife-batterers were the army of occupation. In her study of battered women Susan Brooks Thistlethwaite writes:

> The seeds of wife-beating lie in the subordination of females and in their subjection to male control. This relationship between women and men has been institutionalised in the structure of the patriarchal family and is supported by a belief system, *including a religious one* [italics mine] that makes such relationships seem natural, morally just, sacred.

Thistlethwaite quotes a chilling riposte of a Christian wife-beater to his wife's pleas: "your bones are my bones – just like it says in the Bible".[12] She concluded that religious women were, initially at any rate, more likely to have internalized their oppression: to collude in "justifications" of rape and violence against them that they "asked for it" by provoking the man or men to whom God had given "rule over" them. This century's feminism has, we could say, completed the critical deconstruction of Christian monogamy.

Its reconstruction is by no means inevitable and I neither expect or wish to see it restored in the ways our early 1990s Church and state would like. But we do now have a broader understanding of sexuality, gender and their social construction in history from which to consider the question than has hitherto been available.

The work of Freud and other twentieth-century thinkers

179

made meaningless the old formulation that sex was something to be "reserved" for procreative heterosexual marriage. While we may chose how, when and with whom to "do" sex, that is, acts of genital intercourse, we cannot control our common human condition of being sexual creatures. It has become common as well as necessary to make the distinction between "sex" and "sexuality". Sex, as defined by James Nelson:

> is a biologically based need which is orientated not only towards procreation but indeed towards pleasure and tension release. It aims at genital activity culminating in orgasm. While sex usually is infused with a variety of human and religious meanings, the focus is upon erotic phenomena of a largely genital nature.

Sexuality, while it includes sex, goes beyond it: it is "not the whole of our personhood but it is a very basic dimension of our personhood".[13] While our sexuality does not determine (as Freud believed) all our feelings, thought and actions:

> in ways both obvious and covert it permeates and affects them all ... It includes our appropriation of attitudes and characteristics which have been culturally defined as masculine and feminine. It includes our attitudes about our own bodies and those of others. Because we are "body-selves", our sexuality constantly reminds each of us of our uniqueness and particularity.[14]

Nelson's *Embodiment* (1979) was a good gift to the churches at a time when they were trying to come to terms with the rapid changes brought about by the pill and the (then ten-year-old) divorce law. He reminded the churches that they were not in the business of "maintaining" marriage and family life. "We are historical creatures, and the radical monotheism of Christian faith would remind us that no finite historical form ought ever to be absolutized." Nelson traces the sources and history of Christian sex-negativity and the consequent failure of the Church to develop a real sexual theology on which to project its ethical teaching:

> Few would doubt that this is a time of transition in our understanding of human sexuality. The confusion about sexual mores is the more obvious evidence of this. But there is something else. For too long the bulk of Christian reflection has asked an entirely one-directional question: what does the Christian faith have to say about our lives as sexual beings? Now we are beginning to realise that the enterprise must be a genuinely two directional affair. The first question is essential and we must continue unfailingly to press it. But at the same time it must be joined by, indeed interwoven with, a companion query: What does our experience as sexual human beings mean for the way in which we understand and attempt to live out the faith? What does it mean that we as body selves are invited to participate in the reality of God?[15]

Christian feminists perceive the sexist limitations of Christian thought and life as enemies of a truly embodied, sexual theology. Our claims to a self-defined spirituality and our insistence on naming the she-ness of God have given an important theological dimension to the struggle of women everywhere to reclaim their own sexual bodies.

Mainstream feminism of the early 1970s had little interest in this connection – words like "spirituality" can and do release negative feeling, among woman who see the historical Church as women's enemy; still less in pressing questions of marital morality. The gulf between women's experience of marriage and male-constructed ideology often seems un-bridgeable.

But there are important, visible signs that barriers, both between women and between "interest groups" are everywhere breaking down. As we found out more and more about our feminist past we found that both our radical analyses and our sisterly *solidaire* were often more boldly expressed by our foremothers than by ourselves. In Victorian times "womanly qualities" had not been, as we had assumed on the basis of our own cultural experience (and some considerable prejudice against Victorian sexual repression), enclosed in the home. Though there is no conceivable reason why we should marry a Victorian or any other husband, perhaps there were aspects of Victorian women's "traditional role" as moral reformers we might wish to reclaim. Anyway it became clear that better jobs-for-the-girls reformist feminism was not going to challenge patriarchy. The new, high-powered executive woman was required to conform to a male-defined executive culture; profit-motivated, pragmatic, competitive and morally neutral.

Many if not most of our radical foremothers had been Christian. As we look further back we are, willy nilly, talking about women's Christian past. It became impossible to see the history of women's culture solely in terms of post-Enlightenment consciousness. As suggested in chapter 3 women, orthodox and heretical, had succeeded in creating powerful centres of resistance against male-controlled theocracy. These are increasingly seen by religious and secular feminists alike as part of our common and eminently "usable" past. A consensus seems to be emerging in the movement that religious feminism has a particular area of unfinished business to complete – the reformation of the family that our nineteenth-century foremothers began.

Though many women came to see themselves as losers in the loaded game of 1960s permissiveness, it had, as Beatrix Campbell has pointed out, opened up an important political sexual space. Intimations that women's experience of sex – emotional, spiritual, even physical – was radically different to men's came out of wrestling with the ambiguities of sexual freedom. This space up to the mid-sixties had been available only to a vanguard of the very rich or ultra-bohemian. The widespread availabilty of contraception and society's more relaxed, tolerant attitudes towards extra-marital sex made it possible for ordinary women to refuse to be alienated from their bodies. They may well have to continue to suffer from being loved and left, but now at least they were somewhat less likely to be left (unless they chose) holding the baby or with a "reputation" as used goods: both powerful reasons for saying no. In her popular, provocative book on women and evolution Elaine Morgan predicted a sunnier future for all humanity on the basis of these changes:

> Children are less likely to be born as a result of a woman's being "swept off her feet" by an excess of passion. She can afford to get swept off her feet with joyous abandon for a year or so and still wait before cementing the bond with a couple of children, to see whether the partnership looks like settling down comfortably for a long run; and the qualifications for this are somewhat different. It calls for less of sexiness on the male's part and more of loving kindness. Men who possess most of this quality will be the likeliest to perpetuate their kind and help to form their children's minds.[16]

We know now it is not going to happen as easily as that. The "new man", in so far as he exists outside the media, is a very diffident, culturally beleaguered creature. But Morgan's is a fair summary of what many people hoped would happen. Legions of mothers declared their daughters to be better off than they had been and it is worth recalling the optimism of an era which is now everywhere discredited as dangerously and mindlessly self-indulgent. As the Catholic writer Rosemary Haughton observes, "the mistakes were necessary, in the curious way in which such things work, because it was only by exaggerating, in good faith, some aspect of human sexuality that the real nature of that aspect could be fully seen and later properly appreciated".[17]

Peter Brown and others have shown us the extent to which all social and sexual values were "up for grabs" in the first century of the Christian era. "All things are lawful for me," wrote Paul to the Corinthians. They had to learn for themselves, through the Spirit, which things were also edifying, and so do we. Few believed, in the 1960s that freedom was going to be easy!

Equality of sexual opportunity does not automatically lead to emotional parity any more than it reflects political equality. The pain of unrequited love may well be sharper if the beloved has given and received the body but withheld the heart.

Are women more likely than men to feel this way and choose to be vulnerable and trusting in situations in which they are doomed to disappointment? It really would seem so; the psychologists as well as the poets are agreed on women's primary need for relationality in all things.[19] It has not always served women well, but now at least we have developed a degree of autonomy, sexual and social, which makes it possible to stress our *capacity* for relationality rather than our desperate *need* for it. In our culture, with its veneration of self-reliance, need can be synonymous with inadequacy and clinging dependence.

One of the ways in which women have been made dependent in patriarchal society is through childbearing. While we may find ourselves physically able to detach sex from its consequences of childbirth with some degree of reliability, psychically this is not so easy. But here again, after three millenia, women are reclaiming fertility-as-power. We do not have to believe that childbirth is the only or true purpose of intercourse in order to acknowledge that it is a natural outcome of it and that a woman's body, equipped for this outcome, is a source of knowledge, power and wholeness. The vagina is more than a receiver of the penis, it is the gateway to all human life. A woman's breasts are more than erogenous zones, men for the use of, they are the source of the first human food. Birthing and suckling can be a source of sexual pleasure as well as deepening the mother's bond with her child. Women's sexual pleasure, then, derives less from specific sex acts than from a generalized body response to tenderness. But this experience is not restricted to motherhood. A growing understanding of female libido, as diffuse, autonomous, multi-pleasured physicality, has far-reaching theological implications. It can, of course, lead to the elimination of men as unnecessary or, as Mary Grey suggests in her eloquent and inspiring *Redeeming the Dream*,[19] to a more redemptive mutuality between women and men. Either way, as Linda Hurcombe points out, criticisms of our sex-obsessed culture "should more correctly be qualified as a culture obsessed with *male* orgasm and definitions of the erotic."[20] Perhaps we are not so much demanding "less of sexiness" from men but more of sexiness of and for ourselves!

This anyway was the message of a whole host of 1970s feminist literature urging women to stop despising their bodies – as men do – and come to know and love them.

Women began to envisage a practice of sexual freedom fundamentally different from the joyless exploitative permissiveness they had settled for. Germaine Greer, one of the most spirited pioneer deconstructors of monogamy, was one of those who on her own testimony embraced, with joy, the chance to be "promiscuous" – her word, not mine. She defends this promiscuity, not as hedonism but as a natural outgrowth of "a self-realizing personality" whose

responses are geared to the present and not to nostalgia or anticipation. Although they do not serve religion out of guilt or fear or any sort of compulsion, the religious experience, in Freud's term the *oceanic feeling*, is easier for them to obtain than for the conventionally religious. The essential factor in self-realisation is independent resistance to enculturation.[21]

Greer goes on to examine the divergent implications of enculturation for men and women. Although, like Campbell, she doubts whether the boys actually wanted us to have the sexual freedom they did, she urges women to stay with it and hold out for their own integrity as self-realizing sexual beings, to be both independent and vulnerable.

How? Greer's argument begs more questions than it answers. Though she has revised and expanded her theories she still has little sympathy for the religious, conventional or otherwise. But it is often the case that some of the best food for theological speculation is provided by the opposition. Her central point about enculturation is well taken. As one who obeys the Church's rules it is salutary for me to ask myself whether I do so out of Christian conviction or timid conformity. I find I have no wish to teach my children the facts of life I grew up with: that "serious" relationships were those which saw settled domesticity as their omega point. Nor do I wish to deny that lovingness grown through many different relationships, of which some will and should be sexual, is no less good and holy than lovingness grown through one.

The New Testament teaches the "one flesh" (*henosis*) significance of heterosexual intercourse. Christian tradition as a whole affirms that wherever the unitive and procreative purposes of sex are joined the act – however solemnly or lightly it is undertaken – carries both purposes within itself and is thus irrevocable, indelible. Behaviour labelled "promiscuous" in our culture is presumed to deny this awesome dimension. History would suggest that this holds true for promiscuous men. Women, however, now they are no longer obliged to conceal a sexually active "past", seem less inclined to deny it; more prepared to acknowledge the ways sexual encounters, for good or ill, shape our past and present selves.

The Protestant Church has, by and large, come to terms with the modern pattern of serial monogamy: second marriage in church can function as a sign of forgivenness, a clean slate and a new start. Greer condemns this pattern not for its laxity but for insitutionalizing sexual disloyalty and denial; for her it is obscene legally to replace an old lover with a new. It is a circular rather than a linear promiscuity that she commends. While we may not share her conviction that "lovers who are free to come and go continue to love each other" or that "lovers who are free to change" – which they cannot be, Greer maintains, in most marriages – "remain interesting" she reminds us that openness and growth rather than legality or longevity should be the hallmark of Christian unions.

Can we honestly claim that marriage can, let alone should, provide "security", emotional or economic. It never did and now for sure it never will. Why should an atheistic age delude itself with a sacramental sign which has no value at all for non-Christians?

> It would be better for all concerned if the contractual nature of marriage were a little clearer: If marriage were a contract with safeguards and indemnities indicated in it, it would still not provide emotional security. Its value would be in that it *did not appear to provide it*, so that women would not be encouraged to rely absolutely upon a situation which has no intrinsic permanence.[22]

Agreed. Perhaps when this suggestion is properly implemented – and it is being so by more and more people – and respected instead of being seen as a mercenary second best to "proper" marriages, then those of us for whom the sacramental sign is meaningful – which is precisely as a sign not a security blanket – can begin to reclaim its integrity. Nineteenth-century reformers like Mill fought on behalf of the agnostic minority against the Church's monopoly of marriage rites. Christians who declare themselves appalled by declining standards in marriage today might consider making an effective witness by doing likewise and refusing to sign on with the state. As "the children of saints" why "be joined together like the heathen"?

If it is possible to pursue a healthier, more honest model of sexual plurality can we not also envisage a liberated Christian feminist monogamy?

If we really want to reach out to the casualties of the system we must. Susan Brooks Thistlethwaite's experience with battered women (see above) confirms Freidan's earlier observation that it is harder for women of religious backgrounds to break free of marital oppression. *Henosis* can become a life sentence and in situations where it has become a justification for the partner's life-threatening behaviour women's integrity, indeed survival, lies in getting out from under. If she attempts to do this she may well be condemned by her Church; her pastor may well tell her that the Bible forbids protest and urge her instead to follow Jesus in forgiveness and self-sacrifice. Thistlethwaite's survey shows that Bible study can be a powerful tool for transformation for such women. Lenore Walker, who also works with battered women, observes that once women allow their Bible faith to work for them instead of against them they realize the righteousness of their anger and achieve a greater degree of self-esteem and control of their lives than those not similarly "handicapped". Of course biblical texts can be contradictory. Thistlethwaite has found Luke 9: 1–5, where Christians are told to "shake the dust" from their feet in a futile situation – to be the most "useful text" for abused women. Not so Christ's command to "turn the other cheek"! But why should some texts be thought particularly binding on women? Men do not proceed on material "about" or addressed "to" them. Biblical faith is judged by its fruits; by our ability to seek the will and word of God for our situation. Nowhere in the Bible is sexual righteousness seen in terms of "keeping the home together" at all costs. We are called to peace, to love and to hope and to these ends God may well call us – and women particularly – out of marriage. The Church had no trouble with this idea in the first four centuries of its life.

Historically, though, monogamy has been part and parcel of the best deal we can wrest from men. The Church has colluded in this thinking by allowing its marital rules to be seen as the generous gift of good upright men to the weaker sex. We can remind ourselves of the conventional wisdom Greer and other women urge us to reject by this statement from our famous sexist "protector" C. S. Lewis:

> Women are more naturally monogamous than men. It is a biological necessity. When promiscuity prevails, they will always be more often the victims than the culprits. Also domestic happiness is more necessary to them than to us, and the quality by which they most easily hold a man, their beauty, decreases every year after they come to maturity.[23]

Really? This feels ominously like blackmail. The better-preserved gent will withdraw his investment in unnecessary domestic happiness unless we "hold" him; presumably by placing his self-esteem at the centre of our existence rather than the challenges to growth a shared life can offer. Yet it can be seductive. Traditional Christian moralists were quick to see that women were not well served by permissiveness. However, their protectiveness did not, except in the most superficial way, call for male sexuality itself to be redeemed. Having had such apparent difficulty in seeing the holiness of their own sexual desires, the possibility that God's nature may be shown forth more completely in ours is conceded only with enormous ambiguity, if ever. That is why the "feminine" has been so suppressed in Christian language. But women bear the image and grace of God, as do men. God cannot be labelled and parcelled out in the service of some tired sexual status quo or tamed by "domestic happiness". God's restless curiosity and creativity belong to us too, as much as the sturdy, homely dependability and changelessness men would assign to us for safe keeping.

The debased romanticism which our culture loads on to marriage has been a primary means of taming women (and to be fair to C. S. Lewis he protests the perversion of Romance as vigorously as anyone). Romantic love rang the death knell on any sense of marriage as a communal interest, a social contract. It yields the same result as the arranged marriages it subverted in its early days: domesticity (you start by sinking into his arms and end up with your arms in his sink); but a domesticity accompanied by the dangerous delusion of "choice" and a destructive guilt and grief when the magic wears off. "Falling in love" operates as a psychic tripwire placed across liberated sexuality.

But "falling in love", getting swept off our feet, is part of the air we breathe and we do it whether we will or no. In an essay encouragingly entitled, "Really being in love means wanting to live in a different world",[24] Lucy Goodison proposes a feminist reclamation of romance:

> Should we struggle against these tendencies and feelings in ourselves as counter-productive? I don't think so. Rather, I feel, we should take that power and vitality and work with them. If we were not damaged, if our life experiences had been different, perhaps our loving would not be shot through with need, pain and obsession. But we are as we are and we have to start from here. Rather than denigrating falling in love, we could see it as a healthy response to a crazy world and perhaps one of the stratagems our organism uses to survive. It can act as a beam of light which

can cut through the crap, which reveals the mediocrity, hypocrisy and banality of so much of our society.

I am too addicted to Romance (as so satisfyingly defined by Goodison) to be entirely satisfied with Elaine Morgan's proposal that being "swept off our feet" is something to get out of the way before settling down. It is a bit too close for comfort to the old idea that sexual passion could *only* exist apart from marriage. Can we allow Romance back in without becoming the victims of either its banality or morbidity? For there surely is, for some, a *kairos*, a sense that "now is the appointed time" which presses lovers to make a commitment till death. We somehow know that it will take that long to grow into the present moment. For me the knowledge was suprising, almost shocking and not the least bit sentimental. To recognize and act authentically upon this "now", which for Christians must mean sacramental marriage, needs a grace not readily available in a society obsessed with institutionalized security and couple-ism. (I honestly think that my own marriage would have been impoverished if I had not, by dint of living in larger-than-family households, been fortunate enough to be spared many of the perversions of modern nuclear family life.)

Another way our society trivializes and distorts passion is by exaggerating sexual difference: the manly hero of Romance is "complemented" by his "other half", his Platonic opposite, the truly feminine but ultimately passive heroine. Femininity is presumed to rest heavily upon physical beauty. Plainness, like equality, does not go with our culture's perceptions of "really being in love". In an essay on Emily Brontë's *Wuthering Heights*, that enduring *liebestod* of Victorian fiction, the feminist critic Andrea Dworkin takes issue:

The love story of Catherine Earnshaw and the outcast child Heathcliffe has one point: they are the same, they have one soul, one nature. Each knows the other because each is the other. ("Whatever our souls are made of, his and mine are the same," says Cathy.) Together they are human, a human whole, the self twice over. This says Brontë, is passionate love, real love, unalterable love, not the socialised conflicts and antagonisms of opposites but the deep sameness of two roaming, wild, restless souls.

For Dworkin, Cathy's betrayal is precisely congruent with becoming "feminine". Her femininity "is a slow lazy spoiled abandonment of self".[25]

Is this, I wonder, what Adam wanted when he asked God to replace Lilith with Eve?

For Dworkin, Christianity has been instrumental in maintaining sexual "antagonisms" by its exaltation of "altruistic, self-sacrificing love, Christian "self-effacement and self-denial" and, of course, by assigning these virtues to "real", that is, feminine women.

For Raymond Williams,[26] Heathcliffe and Cathy's love is not, as it would appear in Dworkin's argument, antithetical to religion, it is itself a love which persists in an "experienced transcendence". Nor is it, as Dworkin claims, "greedy, hard and proud". Far from being a macho, anarchic hero created to strike fear and delight into the hearts of Victorian ladies and panting schoolgirls, Heathcliffe is an ordinary man; an Adam in a pre-capitalist Eden. "What he feels is so ordinary that we need no special terms for it. It is that finding of reality in the being of another which is the necessary human identity: the identity of the human beyond the creature." Cathy's bond with Heathcliffe, her sense of his absolute presence, absolute existence in her and hers in him is also an ordinary, though a transforming experience. Heathcliffe does not "thrill" her, he is no more a pleasure to her than she is to herself. He does not sweep her off her feet, he is just there, in her mind, and "if all else perished and *he* remained, *I* should still continue to be." But this love is not anti-social, says Williams, "its quality as given is where social and personal, one's self and others, grow from a single root".

Is this what Héloïse tried to teach Abelard – and the Church?

Cathy does not betray this love in order to settle down to the real world: she betrays it for "the plausible world", for the temporary, the superficial and the pleasing. "Cathy believes she can hold on to a double identity – the profound and the necessary but also the contingent reality."

Reading Williams I was struck by the fact that the terms he uses are precisely those on which two of this century's most prominent radicals, Jean-Paul Sartre and Simone de Beauvoir, defended their sexual politics. De Beauvoir describes how she and Jean-Paul Sartre agreed at the start of their relationship that each would be the most important person for the other. Their love was "necessary"; but this would not preclude them from having other contingent affairs. Now this may have been plausible and pleasing to them but how edifying it was to the contingent objects of their sexual attentions is another question, which Sue Cartledge takes up in "Duty and desire: creating a feminist morality"[27] "Her use of the word 'affairs' for these other lovers is significant. For it is clear from her autobiographical writings that some lovers, both hers and Sartre's, resented their automatic second place." The sexual/emotional hierarchicalism implicit in this arrangement seems to me just as invidious as the Us and Them, backs-against-the-world attitude we find in the worst kinds of marriage; the kind Greer and the historically-rooted left, as represented by Williams, quite rightly denounce.

These days resentful second-besters escape Brontëan tragedy but their indignities are real enough. The sexual objectification of "others", whether by word or deed, is something Christians, in the eyes of whose God nobody can ever be a second-best anything, should always protest. The very tabloid journalism now promoting monogamy as the coming thing of the 1990s does so by de-humanizing those that subvert the new orthodoxy. They have long abandoned high-minded tolerance for low innuendo; a younger mistress, for example, is commonly named a "Bimbo", connoting mercenariness, moral and intellectual cretinousness. The line between a contingent relationship and a despised one would seem to be very thin these days.

Objectification, or to use Buber's language when the I/it relationship prevails over the I/Thou, is the enemy of sexual racial and social justice. And, it is increasingly realized, of ecological justice. When we despise and reject the "other" – that which is not me or mine, us or ours – we exploit it. And we have done this to the earth itself. The term for this pervasive alienation/rejection of the other is dualism; the old Christian heresy which has, again and again, as I have tried to show in this book, masqueraded either as "holiness" or in more recent history as scientific enlightenment. Divesting the human, sexual body of holiness is a primary undergirding mode of dualism, and one which Christian thought is specifically guilty of perpetuating. Theologians bear a heavy and particular responsibility in this regard which they are beginning to work through. Feminists, environmentalists, peace workers have made common cause with one another in seeking a new synthesis of secular and religious prophetism. This means, in the words of one *Sex and God* contributor:

reclaiming the erotic as power from within, as empowerment. The erotic can become the bridge that connects feeling with doing; it can infuse our sense of mastery and control with emotion so that it becomes life-serving instead of destructive. In the dialectic of merging and separating, the erotic can confirm our uniqueness while affirming our deep oneness with all being. It is the realm in which the spiritual, the political and the personal come together[28]

While I hope I have argued for the God-given connections between sexual, social and creational integrity, it would be absurd to suppose that the planet will be saved by the Church getting its theology right – at last. It is God, not right-thinkingness on our part, that will reclaim the earth for us. God works his/her purposes through Creation itself, human and natural, through human hearts, through our human longing for wholeness and meaning.

Human beings can and do find a "given transcendence", a knowledge of holiness through sexual love. It can be a primary way of identifying and celebrating our oneness with all life. As Lucy Goodison writes: "Falling in love may have become unusually important as one of our few routes to an experience of the transcendent. It has been understood as a distortion of a deep urge to love the world which through social pressure gets funnelled into one person."[29] Delete the negatives of "distortion" and "social pressure" and there is the classic apologia for incarnational Christianity. Scandalous particularity. But we should not deny the negatives. Goodison perceives our culture as denying "spirituality outside the confines of established religion". Add to this the privatisation of sex ethics, sexism itself, a romantic myth which consciously stands against rationality; all these have weighed particularly heavily against women.

Environmental concerns have assumed an unprecedented prominence today. Though the crisis we face is of awesome magnitude, it is at the same time highly visible and accessible; manifest in local as well as global issues. Thus it is one in which each of us can participate through our everyday lives and do something about. What is true of the earth is true in microcosm of our sexual bodies. Ecological havoc has taught we cannot use the earth as we will: the AIDS crisis is telling us the same of our individual bodies. In the name of sexual freedom we have polluted them with chemicals just as we have polluted our cities with industrial filth (in which we must include the squalor of a multi-billion pound pornography industry).

Global ecological havoc has been largely brought about through colonialism. We are only just beginning to acknowledge the heavy toll of this in terms of the natural and cultural resources of those the North has dispossessed for private gain. But there is an important sexual dimension to this which we also need to recognize. As Germaine Greer demonstrated in her controversial book on fertility,[30] we have also undermined the sexual integrity of the world's poorer, gentler people. We continue to do so today by intervention in "their" population problem. More and more people are questioning the commercialization and deification of sex in terms of the rigid fertility control we practise to pursue it and which we also export all over the world on the assumption that "they" want the sexual fulfilment we "enjoy" when in fact the opposite is the case. "They", unlike us. have long learned to knit the "wild strand" of sexuality into their social fabric.

Just as we realize that it is no longer enough to honour and celebrate "nature" by embracing enlightened "new age" Greenness, neither can we be content with "celebrating" sex from the safety of our privileged playgrounds. Theological language is particularly *useful* here: Christian teaching of the sacramentality of sex militates against the quasi-mystic sacralizing of sex. Sacramentality is about honouring ordinariness. "Everything begins in mysticism and ends in politics" and at some point we have to come down to basics to put limits and order on things: pursue paths of self-denial, say no to this and yes to that. Monogamy is one such path. God seems to have directed us towards it as the place where the human quest for happiness intersects with the need – expressed by one of Iris Murdoch's heroes – "to learn to be good". For some of us it really is better to marry than burn, because it saves the precious commodity of energy. But if monogamous marriage is the vocation the Church claims it to be, the Church should start teaching it as such, not as the "natural answer" to AIDS. It is a God-given vocation, not a natural one – for either sex.

And there are others. To explore the question of monogamy more deeply we would do well to see what it means for those people who have been denied it spiritually and socially: gay people. While some gay people would resent the imposition of heterosexist "rules" and constructs on their lives, many others – most in fact of my own gay friends – wish to see their unions affirmed by society. The *kairos* experience I spoke of earlier, along with all the pains and joys of sexual love, happens to gay as well as straight lovers. For gay people, too, the impulse to act upon the "now" is real and urgent. Gay Christians are asking for more than tolerance and understanding (though even these are in notably short supply at present), they are asking for the Church's formal blessing on their unions. The pledge to fidelity and permanence forms the central platform of the case for gay marriage. The Church must answer that case.

This is not a question I can ignore. It comes at the end because I have tried to be chronological, that is, to raise questions as they have arisen in their historical context, and it is only in very recent times that questions of Gay Rights/Rites have come to public prominence. But this is no issue to be tacked on to the end, it takes us round to the beginning. A sexual ethic that does not encompass the integrity of gay people is not one I find worth pursuing at all.

I am not gay; for this and other reasons it would be impertinent for me to speak for gay people at this time. In so far as I can and do feel solidarity it is with my gay women friends who have a separate history (of cultural invisibility) from that of gay men. I have throughout this book spoken for and within biblical tradition which has oppressed gay people and repentance is the only appropriate response. I do not believe, as it happens, that the Bible forbids homosexual relations because I do not see that it addresses the question of homosexual orientation at all, but that is not the issue here. The Bible *does* teach us that God is a suffering God and that the divine word comes to us, in each generation, through those who have been brought low in the eyes of the world. The cornerstone the builders reject is that upon which the kingdom is built. Alice Walker, a black woman who has confronted the ugly face of oppression all her life – and stared it down – offers this healing word from her gay friends in San Francisco:

> There was something cheering to the soul about these men, all colours, classes and conditions who in spite of everything they had been taught steadfastly affirmed their right to love each other. And to be open and frolicsome about it. I came to understand why homosexual men are called "gay". Now I hear on the news that one of every two gays in San Francisco has AIDS. Many are dying. In this crisis the gay community has shown courage and tenderness equal to its former raunchiness; the city itself has been compassionate and brave ... So many cultures have died it is hard to contemplate the possible loss or dulling over of another one, or to accept the fact that once again those of us who can appreciate all ... of life will be visually, spiritually and emotionally deprived.[31]

I say amen to that. But I would wish to add that the road from unfallen bliss to wrestling with limitation and finitude, with the knowledge of good and evil, is an honourable one – no human creature can bypass it and remain human. But let us not press the "despised and rejected" metaphor too far: there is nothing "good" about suffering. Jesus has done it for us: it is Finished. We are commanded to seek, by every means open to us, health for the afflicted.

"Why and how does the word become flesh ... Why and how does our flesh become words about the word?" asks Nelson.[33] In an unpublished lecture to the Gay Christian Movement in 1984 Sheila Briggs, a black Roman Catholic theologian, offered a new word on the traditional doctrine of the Trinity. In the belief that human sexuality is made in and corresponds to the reality we call God, Briggs proposed we envision God, in the first person of the Trinity, as a parable of heterosexuality. God is the Creator who calls another out of existence and loves it. This relationship is expressed in the beloved "otherness" of Creator and Creation. But if we stop there, as a heterosexist society would have us do, if we limit our naming and loving to this alone, we lose the fullness of the Word made flesh. We become, in Briggs' words, "sexual Unitarians". God continues, as redeemer and sanctifier (Son/ Spirit) to make and keep the world. Redemption through sameness is the heart of the Christian revelation. Gay people have a particular way of showing forth this aspect of the Three-in-One. Feminism too realizes the uniqueness of love and solidarity between those who have shared the common past, as daughters – as females in a male-dominated world. God so loved the world that she or he gave God's own to be "one of us". Gay sexuality underlines the libido's function of knowledge.

Briggs tantalizingly left us to explore the third part of the Trinity for ourselves. But then so did God! We can move, like Briggs "from remembering to invention" for the spirit blows where it will, through marriage, celibacy, sisterhood, connecting all the opposite poles of our sexual and human experience. The oceanic dimension.

In this oceanic space the soul soars free and love flows unimpeded by fear and ignorance. What is it then that we require of God, God who is within and beyond all longing? That she or he loves us, uniquely, wholeheartedly and for ever and will never turn away. My God is not a harem master or a Great Mother mistress of heaven with an order of favourites. She or he is the one who knows my name. Can we not at least begin to think of monogamy, sexual exclusivity not as prudent conformity – doing what the Church, society or even our loved ones require of us – but as a way of being-in-God?

Notes

CHAPTER 1   A JEALOUS GOD

1   Friedrich Engels, *The Origin and History of the Family, Private Property and the State* (1884), in Karl Marx and Friedrich Engels, *Selected Works*, 3 vols (Progress Publishers, Moscow, 1970), vol. 3, p. 233.

2   Kate Millett, *Sexual Politics* (Virago, 1977), p. 52.

3   Adrienne Rich, *Of Woman Born: Motherhood as Experience and Institution* (Virago, 1977), p. 93. Engels, along with many of his late-Victorian contemporaries, believed that there had once existed a true, universal matriarchy (hence his description of monogamy in terms of "a world historic defeat of the female sex"). While there are no primary sources to back this claim there is a mass of documented evidence of a pre-monogamous stage of human sexual organization. Feminist scholarship is cautious in its approach to matriarchalist speculation. As Rich writes, "it seems to blot out in its inconclusiveness other and perhaps more catalytic questions about the past", like the one discussed here: monogamy and its connection to pre- and post-patriarchal religious, cultural and social forms.

It should be added here that Western scholarship is far more often marked by a cultural bias towards the "inevitability of patriarchy". For example, Bronislaw Malinowski, an anthropologist whose work was much in vogue in the 1950s and 1960s, posits the extraordinary generalization that "in *all* human societies moral tradition and the law decree that the group consisting of a woman and her offspring is not a sociologically complete unit", *Sex and Repression in Savage Society* (Humanities, 1927), p. 213.

4   Ibid. p. 60.

5   Ibid. p. 61.

6   See Susanne Heine, *Christianity and the Goddesses* (SCM, 1987), p. 19.

7   Rosemary Radford Ruether, *Sexism and God Talk: Towards a Feminist Theology* (Boston, Beacon, 1983), pp. 49–50.

8   Sara Maitland, "Triptych" in *A Book of Spells* (Michael Joseph, 1987), pp. 101–21.

9   Ibid. both quotes from p. 118.

10 Robert C. Walton, ed., *A Source Book of the Bible for Teachers* (SCM, 1970), p. 100.

11 Rosemary Radford Ruether, *Disputed Questions: On Being a Christian*, in *Journeys in Faith* series ed. Robert A.Raines (Abingdon, 1982), p. 34.

12 Phyllis Bird, "Images of Women in the Old Testament" in Ruether, ed. *Religion and Sexism* (Simon and Schuster, NY, 1974), p. 66.

13 Ibid. p. 83.

14 Ruether, *Disputed Questions*, op. cit. p. 32.

15 Angela West, "A faith for feminists" in Jo Garcia and S. Maitland, eds, *Walking on the Water: Women Talk about Spirituality* (Virago, 1983), p. 87.

CHAPTER 2 SCANDALOUS PARTICULARITY: NEW TESTAMENT CHRISTIANITY

1 Matt. 5:32; Mark 10:11–12; Luke 16:18. Matt. 19, quoted here, continues: "Whosoever shall put away his wife, except it be for fornication, and shall marry another, committeth adultery: and whoso marrieth her which is put away doth committ adultery" (19:9; repeated 5:32). Jesus' restrictive clause only appears in Matthew's Gospel, hence it is sometimes referred to as the "Matthean exception". Writing for a society whose law did not – as did the Graeco–Roman law – allow women to initiate divorce proceedings, Matthew underlines the double moral danger in "easy divorce". It will make adulteresses of the women concerned, presumably because they would in that society have to seek protection from other men, either in marriage or in concubinage/ prostitution. The warning does not apply to those whose wives have elected to commit adultery, but it was vital for those – probably the majority – who put away their wives on trumped up charges of adultery or for the kind of insubstantial reasons indicated here.

2 See John 4:7–28. It was to this woman that Jesus first revealed himself as the Christ: "I that speak unto thee am he" (v. 26). "And from that city many of the Samaritans believed on him because of the word of the woman who testified" (v. 39). An equally clear challenge to inclusiveness was issued to Jesus by another astute female foreigner, the Syro–Phoenician woman whose story appears in Mark 7:25–30.

3 Rosemary Radford Ruether, "Church and family in the Scriptures and early Christianity" *New Blackfriars*, January 1984, p. 7. First of a series of five essays on *Church and Family*, January–May 1984.

4   "Blaming the Jews for inventing patriarchy", *Lilith* (Jewish feminist journal) 7, 1980; quoted in Elisabeth Schussler Fiorenza, *In Memory of Her: A Feminist Reconstruction of Christian Origins* (SCM, 1983), p. 106.

5   Ibid. pp. 105–9. This argument is expanded in chapter 4.

6   Rosemary Radford Ruether, "Asceticism and feminism: strange Bedmates" in Linda Hurcombe, ed., *Sex and God: Some Varieties of Women's Religious Experience* (Routledge and Kegan Paul, 1987), p. 223.

7   Peter Brown, *The Body and Society: Men, Women and Sexual Renunciation in Early Christianity* (Columbia University Press, 1986; Faber, 1987), p. xv.

8   Ruether, "Church and family", op. cit. p. 10.

9   Brown, op. cit. p. 28.

10 Ibid. p. 26.

11 Sara Maitland, *A Map of the New Country: Women and Christianity* (RKP, 1983), p. 19.

12 Angela West, *Sex and Salvation: A Christian Feminist Bible Study on Corinthians 6:12–7:39* p. 2. (Available from Christian Women's Information and Resources Centre (CWIRES), Blackfriars, St Giles, Oxford OXY 3LY.)

13 See Charles Williams, *Descent of the Dove: A Short History of the Holy Spirit in the Church* (Faber Religious Book Club, 1939), pp. 12–14. Williams refers to a "lost experiment" in which Christian men and women formed spiritual marriages, which apparently involved sleeping together without intercourse. The practice was abandoned because of the scandal it caused. Williams mourns "the loss so early of a tradition whose departure left the church rather overaware of sex, when it might have been creating a polarity with which sex is only partly coincident". Williams' account is somewhat obscure, but ample evidence that Christianity became widely suspect for allowing close association between the sexes is supplied by Peter Brown. This, for example, from one of the Church's pagan critics: "They recognise each other by secret signs and marks; they fall in love almost before they are acquainted: everywhere they introduced a kind of religious lust, a promiscuous 'brotherhood' and 'sisterhood'" (Brown, op. cit. p. 140). The "pagan conviction that Christians met in order to indulge in sexual promiscuity died hard", adds Brown. A similar kind of "spiritual marriage" experiment, known as bramacharya, was attempted, again within the discipline of traditional sexual morality, by Gandhi and his followers. As a feminist I am intrigued by experiments like these,

which, however short-lived, seem to represent attempts to undercut male-structured social institutions and male perceptions of sexuality.

14 West, *Sex and Salvation*, op cit. p. 5.

15 J. A. T. Robinson, *The Body: A Study in Pauline Theology* (SCM, 1952), p. 9.

16 West, op. cit. p. 3.

17 Ibid. p. 10.

18 The letters – Ephesians and the pastoral epistles – in which Paul appears at his most cautious and conservative are of dubious authenticity. It is now widely believed, for example, that Timothy, which contains the famous passage enjoining women to submissiveness and "silence in the churches" (1 Tim. 2:11–14), was written some decades after Paul's death, with the purpose of adapting Paul's message to a form of (male-dominated) Church organization which had not developed during Paul's own life. See *The New English Bible Companion to the New Testament* (OUP and Cambridge, 1970), p. 617, for a discussion of Ephesians, and pp. 660–3 for the pastoral epistles, that is, Timothy, Titus, Philemon.

19 Charles Williams, op. cit. p. 14.

20 Alan Ecclestone, *Yes to God* (Darton, Longman and Todd, 1975), pp. 92–3.

21 Janet Morley in *Poverty, Chastity and Obedience: The Vows Revisited*. Jubilee lectures, 1986 (Jubilee pamphlet, 1987), p. 33.

CHAPTER 3   THE WAY OF NEGATION

1 Quoted in A. Alvarez, *Life after Marriage: Scenes from Divorce* (Macmillan, 1987), p. 116.

2 Ruether, "Asceticism and feminism" in *Sex and God*, op. cit. p. 229.

3 Ibid. p. 223.

4 The argument continues in this century. Hannah Arendt, for example, denounces Christianity, along with Marxism, as a destructive life philosophy, the antithesis of the Greek way. Echoing Nietzsche, who described Christianity as a "slave morality", Arendt writes: "The old contempt towards the slave who had been despised because he served only life's necessities and submitted to the compulsion of his master because he wanted to stay alive at all costs, could not possibly survive in the Christian era" (*The Human Condition*, University of Chicago Press, 1958, p. 316). Statements like this are not intended as any sort of tribute to Christianity but rather as accusations that Christians'

insidious individualism, shown in their readiness – someone would say masochist lust – to be martyrs, their opting out of sex and marriage, debased the coinage of public life. At the other end of the critical spectrum we find those who accuse Christianity of inculcating docile conformity, of rendering too much "to Caesar". This raises two important questions: first what kind of public life was available to most people before, or during, Rome's decline; secondly were these the only means by which Christians subverted civic order?

Discussing Arendt's position Jean Bethke Elshtain notes that "her real heroes are Greek warriors who died young and left beautiful memories" (*Public Man, Private Woman*, Martin Robertson, Oxford, 1981, p. 58). There is a clue here. We live in a society which, like the Roman world, looks with as much suspicion on pacifism as it does on celibacy, and early Christian pacifism has been underplayed in Christian history. It was the early Christians' refusal to fulfil military as well as marital obligations that brought obloquy and martyrdom upon their heads. By upholding the right of men and women to opt out of both, early Christianity can be said, if not to have actually denied, then to have most clearly and unequivocally redefined "those things that belong to Caesar".

5   Eric Fuchs, *Sexual Desire and Love: Origins and History of the Christian Ethic of Sexuality and Marriage*, (tr. John Ratti Clark, 1983), p. 68.

6   Hennecke and Schneemelcher, *New Testament Apocrypha*, vol. 11 (Philadelphia, Westminster, 1963), pp. 322–90. The *Acts of Paul and Thecla* were already a part of Christian oral tradition by the time the pastoral epistles were written. Though it cannot be proved that 1 Timothy was written specifically to counteract the view of Paul found in the story, it should be evident, as Ruether points out, that the legend of Thecla represents Paul in exactly the opposite stance from that attributed to him in 1 Timothy.

7   Jerome, Epist. xxii. 20, quoted in James Nelson, *Embodiment: An Approach to Sexuality and Christian Theology* (SPCK, 1979), p. 52.

8   West, op. cit. p. 6.

9   Ibid. p. 7.

10 Williams, op. cit. p. 14.

11 Pliny, *Letters and Panegyrics*, xciv, p. 289, quoted in Fuchs, op. cit. p. 88.

12 See Brown, op. cit. pp. 127–39. Brown convincingly exonerates Clement of superspiritualist dualism but suggests that because Clement, who was imbued with "the sharp aesthetic sensibility of a Greek", absorbed the Stoics' hostility to sexual pleasure he "moved the centre of gravity"

further away from the affirmative view of sexual discipline of Judaism and earlier Christianity.

13 Teilhard de Chardin, *Towards the Future* (Collins, 1975), p. 66.

14 Ambrose, *Expos. evang. Sec. Lucam*, Bk. X, no. 161, quoted in Marina Warner, *Joan of Arc: The Image of Female Heroism* (Weidenfeld and Nicolson, 1981; Penguin, 1983), p. 154.

15 See ibid. ch. 7, "Ideal Androgyne", pp. 146–63.

16 Quoted in Alvarez, op. cit. pp. 116–17.

17 *De Sermone Dom in Monte*, 41, quoted in Ruether, "Virginal feminism and the Fathers of the Church", in id. (ed.), *Religion and Sexism*, op. cit. p. 161.

18 Ibid. p. 162.

19 One schismatic extreme, the Donatists, were rigorous purists who wished to separate themselves in worship from the Christians who had "collaborated" with pagans. Against this threat Augustine formulated the precept that the unworthiness of the minister – and recipients – of the sacrament did not hinder its grace since the only and true "minister" was Christ himself. The Pelagians represented an opposite heresy: they denied the reality of sin, believing that Adam only injured himself by his disobedience, that there were sinless men before Christ and that the whole race neither died in Adam nor depended on Christ for their rising again. Both sects can be seen as denying the grace of forgiveness, the Donatists by saying you cannot have it and the Pelagians by saying you do not really need it, man can pull himself up by his own bootstraps; all of which must have been personally as well as administratively painful to Augustine whose faith and authority were, as he saw it, dependent upon his own forgiveness.

20 Williams, op. cit. p. 70.

21 From the fourth century onwards there was a marked revival of the old Hebrew taboos against female impurity. The common belief that Christians should not take Communion the morning following intercourse, that menstruating women should not even enter a church, were not products of early Christianity but arose around the fifth century.

22 C. S. Lewis, *The Allegory of Love: A Study in Medieval Tradition* (OUP, 1936; paperback, 1958), p. 6.

23 Marina Warner, *Alone of All Her Sex: The Myth and Cult of the Virgin Mary*, Weidenfeld and Nicolson, 1976; Quaver, 1978.

24 Ibid. xxi.

25 Ibid. p. 133.

26 Brown, op. cit. p. 446.

27   Warner, *Monuments and Maidens: The Allegory of the Female Form* (Weidenfeld and Nicolson, 1985), p. 189.
28   Ibid. p. 181. See also Sara Maitland, *Passionate Prayer* in *Sex and God*, op. cit., p. 139.
29   Waddell, Peter Abelard, op. cit., p. 76.

CHAPTER 4   ROMANCE

1   Reaffirmed in *Marriage and the Church's Task*. General Synod Marriage Commission Report, 1978.
2   C. S. Lewis, *The Allegory of Love*, op. cit. p. 13.
3   The history of marriage rites is interesting. Old Roman ceremonies were followed without alteration for several centuries, which suggests the Church's radical disinvolvement in any aspect of marital order. The first traces of Christian rites emerge only in the fourth century: not until the ninth century is there any detailed account of Christian nuptials and even then the order is strikingly akin to that of Imperial Rome, which again must have upheld a sense that marriage and sex belonged not to Christ but to the world. Warner in *Alone of All Her Sex* (op. cit. pp. 145–6) suggests that the roots of Tridentine affirmation ran farther back in time than the liturgical history allows for.   By the time of the Fourth Lateran Council in 1215 (referred to in ch. 3) the Church was making concerted efforts to check abuse and prevent casual hasty marriages and elopements by ordering the reading of banns and the public conducting of weddings. To illustrate "the seriousness with which the medieval Popes viewed marriage" Warner cites the example of Pope Eugenius III's dramatic intervention in the divorce petition brought by a Norman count. The Pope dismissed the case "and then his face covered with tears, he leapt down from his throne, in the sight of all, and lay at the feet of the Count so that his mitre rolled in the dust". Eugenius then attempted to reconcile the couple there and then with his own ring. It was at this early date, in Warner's view, that the "seeds of the Western idea of love-in-marriage-until-death-us-do part were sown".
4   C. S. Lewis, op. cit. p. 4.
5   Ibid. p. 17.
6   Warner, op. cit. p. 146.
7   Priestly celibacy was not absolutely imposed until the eleventh century, much later than is commonly supposed. For a brief historical assessment of the struggle and its continuing implications for Catholicism see E. Schillebeeckx, *Ministry* (SCM, 1981), pp. 85–99.

8   C. S. Lewis, *Donne and Love Poetry* in Walter Hooper, ed. *Selected Literary Essays* (Cambridge University Press), p. 117. Lewis sees the hallmarks of Donne's love poetry – its unadorned eroticism, its marked separation from his devotional poems – as derivative of Donne's "Roman Catholic background"; "Donne never for long gets rid of the sense of the sinfulness of sexuality."

9   Lewis' attachment to the Protestant housewifely ideal is manifest throughout his correspondence. In *The Four Loves* (1960) he describes the presence of women "out of their place" in the intellectual sphere as destructive to the delights of male conversation. In *That Hideous Strength* (1945) a young wife is firmly told that her Christian discipleship demands she gives up her thesis and returns to full-time care of her home and husband. For this reminder, my thanks to Margaret Duggan's assessment of Lewis' prodigious influence twenty-five years after his death, in *Church Times*, 18 November 1988.

10   *D. Martin Luther's Werke* etc., (Weimar, 1933), pp. 327–8, quoted in Julia O'Faolain and Lauro Martinez, eds, *Not in God's Image* (Virago, 1979), p. 208. The editors have culled further evidence from his informal conversations of Luther's "biology is destiny arguments". For example, "Men have broad shoulders and narrow hips" and so accordingly possess intelligence; women, vice-versa, were "made to stay at home". And so on ... and on (ibid. pp. 209–11).

11   Quoted in James Nelson, *Embodiment*, op. cit. p. 55. Luther's pronouncements are markedly *un*romantic. Luther was much troubled by the strength of his own sexual urges, which seems to have prevented him from seeing a natural connection between love and fidelity and led him to stress the "hedge against lust" function of marriage far more strongly than his contemporaries.

12   See Sara Maitland, *A Map of the New Country*, op. cit. ch. 3, "Communities of faith", summarizes the history of female orders and offers a useful assessment of their contribution to Christian feminist awareness.

13   Ironically since his own divorce precipitated Reformation events in England, it was Henry VIII who drew up the first British Act of Parliament declaring marriage to be indissoluble. It remained law until the Restoration when divorce by a private Act of Parliament was restored (in 1669).

14   Ruether, "Church and family" op. cit. Part 2 (February 1984), p. 85. Recent feminist history has drawn attention to the extent of witch-hunting across Europe over 400 years as well as the manifest gynaephobia of its perpetrators. The inquisitor's handbook, the *Malleus Malefi-*

carum (Hammer of the Witches), written by two Dominicans, Heinrich Kramer and Jacobus Sprenger, summed up a century of theory and practice. The belief that "when a woman thinks alone she thinks evil" was taken to heart by (Puritan) witch-hunters in the seventeenth century. Knowledge and skill in traditional arts like herbalism, midwifery and folklore – the province of single, independent-minded women – became ever more suspect. Witch hysteria was fanned by the Reformation conflict itself: there were incidents when Papism or Protestantism were seen as evidence of witchcraft – always closely allied to heresy – by the other side.

15 Rosemary Radford Ruether, *To Change the World: Christology and Cultural Criticism* (SCM, 1981), p. 41.
16 Williams, *Descent of the Dove*, op. cit. p. 130.
17 Eleanor McLaughlin, "Equality of souls, inequality of sexes: women in medieval theology", in Ruether, ed. *Religion and Sexism*, op. cit. p. 222.
18 Adrienne Rich, *On Lies, Secrets and Silence: Selected Prose 1966–1978* (Virago, 1980), p. 216.
19 Francis Xavier Murphy, "Petrarch and Christian philosophers" (Lecture, Washington, 1974), quoted in Warner, op. cit. p. 172.
20 Ibid. p. 173.
21 Germaine Greer, *The Female Eunuch* (Paladin, 1971), p. 202.
22 Warner, op. cit. p. 188.
23 Germaine Greer, *Shakespeare*, in *Past Master* series, gen. ed. Keith Thomas (OUP, 1986), p. 109.
24 Ibid. pp. 112–13.
25 Alice Clark, *Working Life of Women in the Seventeenth Century*. Routledge, 1919; RKP, 1982.
26 Charles Williams, *The Image of the City and other Essays* (OUP, 1958), p. 161.

CHAPTER 5 THE RATIONALIST CHALLENGE

1 Veronica Wedgewood, *History and Hope* (Collins, 1987), p. 68.
2 Jeremy Taylor, Sermon XVII.
3 Ibid.
4 Milton *The Doctrine and Discipline of Divorce* (1643; Sherwood, 1920), bk II, p. 70. Despite the disrepute into which this work brought him

Milton continued to plead his case in three more pamphlets over the following two years.

5 Ibid. bk II, p. 62.

6 Lewis H. Berens, *The Digger Movement in the Days of the Commonwealth* (1906), quoted in Antonia Fraser, *The Weaker Vessel: Woman's Lot in Seventeenth-Century England* (Weidenfeld and Nicolson, 1984), p. 233.

7 *Guardian*, 28 April 1989.

8 Mary Astell, *Reflections on Marriage*, 3rd edn, 1706.

9 Wedgewood, op. cit. p. 69.

10 Einstein's theory of relativity has displaced the old Newtonian view of the universe as a machine; patterns have come to light in the field of quantum physics which positively invite metaphysical/mystical interpretation. Recent speculations by reputable physicists have focused on the parallels between quantum phenomena and spirituality: a development which will, it is widely believed, lead to a desecularization of thought with far-reaching implications for all areas of life.

11 Fay Weldon, *Letters to Alice: On First Reading Jane Austen* (Michael Joseph, 1984; Coronet, 1985), p. 35.

12 Quoted in Harriett Gilbert, *A Woman's History of Sex*. Pandora Press (RKP), 1987. Lady Mary Wortley Montague, letterwriter, philanthropist, was praised by Voltaire above all the dazzling women intellectuals of her time.

13 Claire Tomalin, *The Life and Death of Mary Wollstonecraft* (Weidenfeld and Nicolson, 1974; Pelican, 1977), p. 51.

14 Gilbert, op. cit. p. 122.

15 Kate Millett, *Sexual Politics* (Virago, 1969), p. 128.

16 Adrienne Rich, *On Lies, Secrets and Silence: Selected Prose 1969–1978* (Virago, 1980), p. 11.

17 Barbara Taylor, *Eve and the New Jerusalem: Socialism and Feminism in the 19th Century*, pp. 248–60.

18 Millett, op. cit. p. 70.

19 Evidence to the Royal Commission (comprising 25 men) set up in 1870 to investigate the working of the CDAs (18 March 1871).

20 Florence Nightingale, *Cassandra*, quoted in Elizabeth Longford, *Eminent Victorian Women* (Papermac, 1982), p. 115.

21 Weldon, op. cit. p. 42.

22 Phyllis Rose, *Parallel Lives: Five Victorian Marriages*, Chatto and Windus, 1984.

CHAPTER 6 SNAKES AND LADDERS

1 Doris Lessing *To Room 19*, in her *Collected Short Stories*, 2 vols, Heineman, 1978; also in Malcolm Bradbury, ed., *Penguin Book of Modern British Short Stories*, (1963), p. 151.

2 Quoted in Alvarez, *Life After Marriage*, op. cit. p. 22. Stone's assessment is somewhat misleading. It was wives' deaths, notably in childbirth, that brought many marriages to an end. Maternal mortality rose to unprecedented levels with the appearance of childbed (puerperal) fever in the early eighteenth century.

3 See Jessie Bernard, *The Future of Marriage*, Penguin, 1972. In her postscript, Bernard describes her reluctant conversion to feminism when her researches showed that married men were happier, healthier than single men and that the opposite was the case of women, particularly those who were full-time home makers.

4 George Eliot, *Middlemarch* (1871; Penguin, 1965), p. 896.

5 Betty Friedan, *The Feminine Mystique* (Penguin, 1965), pp. 273–4.

6 Kate Millet, *Sexual Politics*, op. cit. p. 171. Millet writes that by the 1930s and 1940s the zeal of Soviet "pro-family" propaganda "was indistinguishable from that of other Western nations including Nazi Germany"; see also n. 10.

7 Beatrix Campbell, "A feminist sexual politics: now you see it now you don't", *Feminist Review*, no. 5, 1980; repr. in Mary Evans, ed., *The Woman Question: Readings on the Subordination of Women* (Fontana, 1982), p. 126.

8 Ibid.

9 Raymond Williams, *The English Novel from Dickens to Lawrence* (Granada Paladin, 1970), p. 74.

10 Virginia Woolf, *Three Guineas*, (Hogarth, 1938; Penguin, 1977), p. 162. Woolf explores the connection between the political repressiveness of fascism and sexism. Both exaggerate sexual difference by venerating men as warriors and protectors of "their" women.

11 Campbell, op. cit. p. 127.

12 Susan Brooks Thistlethwaite, "Battered women and Interpretation" in Letty Russel, ed., *Feminist Interpretation of the Bible* (Blackwell, 1985), p. 97.

13 Nelson, *Embodiment*, op. cit. p. 18.

14 Ibid. p. 133.

15 Ibid. pp. 8–9.

16 Elaine Morgan, *The Descent of Woman* (Souvenir, 1972), p. 280.

17 Rosemary Haughton, "The theology of marriage" in Ruth Tiffany

Barnhouse and Urban T. Holmes, eds, *Male and Female: Christian Approaches to Sexuality* (Seabury, 1976), p. 216.

18 See Jean Baker Miller, *Towards a New Psychology of Women* (Beacon, 1976; Pelican, 1978). Miller's perception that most women "stay with, build on, and develop in a context of attachment and affiliation with others" (p. 87) undermines the idea that psychological patterns are laid down in the first six years of life. While women undoubtedly suffer greater stress, depression etc. when relationships are strained or broken, Miller's prognosis is optimistic. Women's capacity for affiliation provides the basis of "a more advanced social existence" (p. 93). She further maintains that "Men are longing for an affiliative mode of living – one that would not mean going back to mother", in the Freudian sense of re-living Oedipal jealousies and conflicts, but rather a way to go on to a "greater human communion". (p. 92).

19 Mary Grey, *Redeeming the Dream* (SPCK, 1989), pp. 162–5.

20 Linda Hurcombe, introd. to *Sex and God*, op. cit. p. 5.

21 Germaine Greer, *The Female Eunich*, op. cit. p. 145. Greer is drawing on the work of the psychologist Abraham Maslow who propounded the idea of a "self actualizing" personality. See also Nelson, op. cit. pp. 95–6, for a more detailed assessment of the sexual characteristics of Maslow's self-realizing persons:they enjoy sex more than the average person; do not set great store by individual sex acts, or by "gender roles" in relationships, are more loving and respectful towards their partners. Greer concludes that "it would be a fluke if such a character were to remain completely monogamous" yet the evidence suggests that such people, though unlikely to "follow the rules" like the "conventionally religious", make good satisfying marriages and are therefore less driven than others to pursue extra-marital affairs. For Nelson Maslow is making "a powerful statement though in secular language about grace ... if (Maslow's) wording sounds too optimistic and lacking in the recognition of our continuing sin, we can nevertheless affirm the truth to which he is pointing".

22 Greer, ibid. p. 242.

23 C. S. Lewis, "We have no right to happiness" (posthumous art.), *Saturday Evening Post*, December 1963; repr. in *God in the Dock: Essays on Theology* (Collins/Fount, 1979), pp. 107–8.

24 Lucy Goodison in Sue Cartledge and Joanna Ryan, eds, *Sex and love: New Thought on Old Contradictions* (Women's Press, 1983), p. 63.

25 Andrea Dworkin in *Letters from a War Zone* (Secker and Warburg, 1984), pp. 69–70.

26 Raymond Williams, op. cit. p. 56.

27 In *Sex and Love*, op. cit. p. 175.
28 Starhawk (Miriam Simos), *Dreaming the Dark: Magic, Sex and Politics* (Beacon, 1982), p. 138.
29 Goodison, op. cit. p. 62.
30 *Sex and Destiny: The Politics of Human Fertility*, Secker and Warburg, 1984; Picador, 1985.
31 Alice Walker, *Living by the Word: Selected Writings 1973–1987* (Women's Press), p. 169.
32 Nelson, op. cit. p. 20.

Index

Index